CW00524376

Health and Social Care
for Intermediate GNVQ

second edition

Mark Walsh and
Josephine de Souza

Published by HarperCollins *Publishers* Limited
77–85 Fulham Palace Road
Hammersmith
London
W6 8JB

www.**Collins**Education.com
On-line support for schools and colleges

First published 2000
Reprinted 2000, 2001

Layout, compilation, design and illustrations © HarperCollins *Publishers* Limited 2000
Text © Mark Walsh and Josephine de Souza 2000

ISBN 0 00 329103 0

British Cataloguing in Publication Data
A cataloguing record for this publication is available from the British Library

Almost all the case studies in this book are factual. However, the persons, locations and subjects have been given different names to protect their identity. The accompanying images are for aesthetic purposes only and are not intended to represent or identify any existing person, location or subject. The publishers cannot accept any responsibility for any consequences resulting from this use, except as expressly provided by law.

Series commissioned by Charis Evans
Edited and typeset by DSM Partnership
Cover designed by Patricia Briggs
Cover picture by Tony Stone Images
Pictures by Helen Evans
Project managed by Kay Wright
Production by Emma Lloyd-Jones
Printed and bound by Scotprint

www.**fire**and**water**.co.uk
The book lover's website

Contents

Acknowledgements

We would like to acknowledge and thank everybody involved in producing and supporting the writing of this book. This includes our colleagues at HarperCollins and DSM for the friendly, supportive way they helped us; the readers of the draft manuscripts for their valuable comments and the students and teachers who've contributed many of
the ideas that have gone into the book.

Mark Walsh and Josephine de Souza

I get most of my support and inspiration
from Karen. This book wouldn't be the same without her.

Mark Walsh

I am grateful to my family for their patience and understanding and to Eula and Cynthia for their comments.

Josephine de Souza

Introduction

Welcome to the second edition of the GNVQ Intermediate Health and Social Care student textbook. Our aim is to provide you with interesting learning material that is easy to follow, so that you can develop and extend your knowledge and understanding of health and social care. This introduction will help you to understand the GNVQ award and explains how to use the book effectively.

Reading through the introduction will help you to understand more about:

- where the GNVQ Intermediate Health and Social Care award fits into the national framework of qualifications
- how the GNVQ Intermediate Health and Social Care award is organised.

You will also learn about:

- the subjects that you will cover in the course
- how to study on the course
- how your work will be assessed
- key skills
- what you might do when you have finished the course.

About GNVQ

What is a GNVQ?

The letters **GNVQ** stand for General National Vocational Qualification.

- **General** – GNVQ courses provide a broad general vocational education focused on a particular area of work, such as health and social care.
- **National** – GNVQ is a national qualification, recognised by colleges and employers all over the country. When you complete the course you will receive your certificate from one of the three bodies (Edexcel, OCR, AQA) which award GNVQ certificates.
- **Vocational** – GNVQ courses are vocational or work related. Your course relates to the world of health and social care work and employment. This is different to GCSE and A level courses which are concerned with academic subjects like history and geography.
- **Qualification** – GNVQ is a qualification or award which recognises your learning and achievement at pass, merit or distinction grade.

So, GNVQs are directly relevant to the world of work and employment. They show that you have the knowledge and skills that employers are looking for. They can also lead on to higher level qualifications, if that is your aim.

What is the GNVQ Intermediate Health and Social Care?

This qualification is called **Intermediate** because it is the middle level of GNVQ qualifications, between the Foundation GNVQ below and the Advanced GNVQ above. The Intermediate standard is about the same as GCSE grades A* to C.

Your GNVQ Intermediate Health and Social Care course will help you learn about:

- the way people develop and change through their lives
- the way people experience health and well-being
- the kinds of health and social problems that people experience
- how the health services and social care services work to prevent and respond to these health and social care problems.

How is the qualification organised?

The GNVQ Intermediate Health and Social Care is made up of six units. For an Intermediate GNVQ full award you must take and pass all six units. Three of the units are compulsory and three are optional. The **compulsory units** are the same for everyone. **Optional units** vary from one awarding body to another and you or your school or college can choose which three you will take. All the units are the same size. If you are studying for Health and Social Care for Part One Intermediate GNVQ, you will only need to cover the three compulsory units.

This book gives you the background knowledge you need for the compulsory units of your GNVQ. It includes many activities to help you with your learning and to assist you in undertaking the written work on which you will be assessed. You should try to do the activities when you come across them, as they are an important way of improving your learning.

What is the course about?

In this book, the activities are styled up in a distinctive manner. The activity opposite, the first in this book, helps you discover what the course is about.

Course specifications

Ask your tutor for a copy of the specifications for the three compulsory units you will be taking. Read through the section of the specification for Unit 1 headed 'About this unit'.

1 Make a list of any six jobs (or main roles) that you have heard of in health and social care. For example, you might include social worker in your list.

2 For each of these jobs, make some notes about what skills the job calls for and what the jobholder would need to know. For example, a social worker would need to be able to judge what sort of care or help someone needs, and to know what is available.

3 For two of the jobs, make some notes about how the jobholder should behave towards the people he or she cares for in the job, and about the kind of behaviour he or she should avoid.

Now look through the next part of the specification headed 'What you need to learn' and see how many of your ideas and notes you can find. What else is in the unit that you hadn't thought of? Can you find these points in the index of this book?

Spend a few minutes looking at the 'About this unit' section of the Unit 2 specification. Try to think of some examples of the points listed in the specification. Ask your tutor to explain any words you don't understand. Do the same for Unit 3.

When you receive a copy of the specifications for the three optional units that you will be studying, remember to read the 'About this unit' sections carefully and spend a few minutes thinking about the contents before you look at the rest of the specification.

How will I learn?

While you will learn a lot from this book, you will also learn a great deal by carrying out your own enquiries and investigations. These will often be a part of an assessment work exercise which counts towards your unit assignment and final result.

You may learn by:

- carrying out research in libraries and resource centres
- visiting care settings and talking to the people who work there and the clients who receive care
- hearing about the experiences of patients, clients and care workers by interviewing them, or by watching films and videos
- using case studies to gain more understanding of what it is like to need or to receive care
- interviewing people who have agreed to help you with your work and write reports about the care they have given or received
- arranging work experience with a local care organisation or provider.

How long is the course?

Normally, you should complete your Intermediate GNVQ in one year of full-time study. However, this is not a fixed time limit and some people may need longer to complete the qualification or might choose to spread their study over a longer period.

How will my work be assessed?

Four of the six units (two compulsory and two optional) will be assessed through your coursework, which you collect in a portfolio. Two units (Unit 3 and one of your optional units) will be assessed by external tests.

What is a portfolio?

A portfolio is the folder in which you keep the work that you have done during the course and which counts towards your result. This work is called your assessment evidence. The portfolio is at the heart of your GNVQ course. Everything in it should be your own work.

What is an external test

External tests are set by your Awarding Body and will assess your skills, knowledge and understanding of unit 3 (Understanding personal development). There will be two opportunities each year to take the external assessment, in

January and in June. The grade you achieve in the external assessment will be your grade for unit 3.

The external tests will be short-answer questions to case study material. Your teacher or tutor will be able to give you more information and help in preparing for the tests by giving you opportunities to practise short-answer questions.

Have a go at tackling the next activity to find out more about assessment evidence.

ACTIVITY

Assessment evidence

Find your copy of the specifications for Unit 1. Look at the section on assessment evidence and at the box called 'What you need to produce'.

- How many reports will you have to write?

- How many health and/or social care settings will you have to study?

- What will you have to describe?

- What will you have to explain?

- What will you have to explore?

Each time you begin work on a new unit that is assessed by portfolio, read the section of the specification headed 'What you need to produce' and spend a few minutes thinking about the assessment evidence that is required.

What grades can I get?

There are three grades: **pass**, **merit** and **distinction**. Look again at the assessment evidence section in the Unit 1 specifications. It has three columns. The first one says all the things you have to do to get a pass. To get a merit, you have to do all the things required for a pass plus the things listed in the second column. For a distinction, you must do everything you have to do for a merit plus the things listed in the third column.

To find out the difference between each grade you need to identify the key words in these columns. They are the ones which, for each bullet point, say what you actually have to do. For example, to achieve a pass in Unit 1, you have to:

- correctly identify …
- clearly describe …
- describe …
- demonstrate …
- describe … .

Look at the key words and phrases in the merit column, and then in the distinction column. You will see that, for these grades, you have to do things which are more difficult than the requirements for a pass.

You will be awarded a pass, merit or distinction for each unit, including the ones in which you take an external test. These results are then added up to give you the grade for the whole qualification. You have to pass every unit to achieve the qualification, but you do not have to get all merits or all distinctions to achieve these grades for the whole qualification.

Who will assess my work?

Normally your tutor will be your **assessor**. He or she will discuss your coursework with you and assess it at the end of each unit. As you work through the course, you will know what standard you are reaching.

Your assessor is supported by an internal verifier. This is another tutor who works at your college or school. His or her job is to check that your assessor is making a fair assessment of the evidence in your portfolio. The awarding body checks that the work being done at your school or college is at the right standard.

The awarding body also marks your external tests.

What will it say on my certificate?

Your final certificate will list all the units you have completed and the grades you achieved for each unit. It will also say what grade you achieved for the whole qualification.

What happens if I don't finish the course?

If you are unable to complete all the units in the course, you will be given a certificate showing which units you have passed, and at what grade.

What can I do when I have finished the course?

When you have gained your Intermediate GNVQ qualification, you can choose between:

- taking a step up the GNVQ ladder (to Advanced GNVQ)
- changing on to the academic route (for example, by taking an A level course)
- getting a job, probably with the opportunity to gain NVQ qualifications at a higher level.

What about key skills?

There are six key skills units. They are the same for everybody, regardless of the qualification they are taking. They are:

- communication
- application of number
- information technology
- working with others
- improving own learning and performance
- problem solving.

Key skills are the skills you need to succeed in your studies and you need when you get a job. They are the skills you need to get things done and to make things happen at work. You use and apply them in real situations (see Figure I.1).

Although you don't have to achieve any key skills units to pass your GNVQ course, all schools and colleges are likely to expect you to aim for at least communication, application of number and information technology. If you achieve these, at any level, you will be awarded a separate key skills qualification.

How are key skills assessed?

Like the GNVQ, key skills are assessed through a combination of portfolio evidence and external tests. Your tutor will explain this to you. If you find that you need some extra help with your key skills, talk to your GNVQ tutor.

Figure I.1: The applications of key skills in real situations

Key skill	Application
Communication	When you are working with clients, you need to be able to communicate one to one; when you are writing a report about a client, you must be able to write clearly and accurately.
Application of number	You will need number skills when you are measuring a child's development, or people's health and fitness, or when you are working out a diet or checking a dose of medicine.
Information and communications technology	You can use your ICT skills to present written work, or to search for information in a database.
Working with others	You have to be able to work with others if you are to make a successful career in health and social care.
Improving own learning and performance	We can all improve how we learn and what we achieve, and we need this skill to ensure that we continue to develop personally and professionally.
Problem solving	We are all faced with problems when studying or at work. You can get better at tackling problems if you work on this skill.

 Build your learning

Summary points

- GNVQ stands for General National Vocational Qualification.

- Health and social care is about people, how they develop, the problems they may experience, and how the health and social care services can help.

- The GNVQ Intermediate Health and Social Care is made up of three compulsory units and three optional units.

- During the course, you will make enquiries, talk to care workers and people receiving care, and learn from several different sources.

- You will complete an assignment for four units, and do an external test for each of the other two units.

- You can achieve a pass, merit or distinction grade.

- You may also achieve up to six key skills units.

Key words and phrases

You should know the meaning of the words and phrases listed below as they relate to your GNVQ course. If you're not sure about any of them, go back through the last eight pages of this introduction to check and refresh your understanding.

- GNVQ
- Intermediate level
- Health and social care

- Compulsory units
- Optional units
- Portfolio
- Assessment evidence

- External test
- Pass, merit, distinction
- Assessor
- Key skills

Student questions

1 What does GNVQ stand for?

2 How many optional units are there in a GNVQ Intermediate Health and Social Care full award?

3 Where can you find out about the contents of the course?

4 What happens if you don't finish the course in a year?

5 How many units are assessed through portfolio evidence?

6 Which is better, a merit grade or a distinction grade?

7 What does an internal verifier do?

8 What are key skills?

About this book

How is this book organised?

Each main section of this book has the same title as one of the three compulsory units in the Intermediate GNVQ specification. Look at the preview to Unit 1 (see pages 2–3) and compare it with the 'About this unit' and 'What you need to learn' sections in the specifications. How do they compare?

You will find that if you make similar comparisons for units 2 and 3 (on pages 82–3 and pages 160–1 respectively), you will see that the book covers the material that you need to learn as set out in the specification for the qualification.

How does the book help me to learn?

The book includes three important features to help you learn and revise.

Activities

As you know, it is always easier to learn something by doing it than by just reading about it or being told about it. You have already done some activities in this introduction, but there are many more throughout the book. For example, have a look at the activity on page 165. Making lists like those asked for in this activity really makes you think about what you are learning. Other activities suggest some research you might do, or points to discuss, or notes to make, or things to think about.

Case studies

Turn to page 17 of the book and read through the case study about working in the Central Area team office. The names of the people in this study have been made up but the situations described are typical. After some of the case studies in the book, you are asked questions or given something to discuss with other people. So, though you probably don't yet have experience of working with real people in care situations, this is the next best thing. You can use the case studies so that when you go out on work placement or get your first job, you have some experience to draw on.

Build your learning

Throughout each unit, you will find a section called 'Build your learning'. In fact, there is one earlier in this introduction. Have a look at the example on pages 32–3 now. These sections include the following features.

- **Summary points.** Use these to check that you have understood all the key points in the section.
- **Key words and phrases.** As you finish each section of the book, you can test your learning by checking that you understand the meaning of key words and phrases. Write down what you think each word or phrase means. Then find where it is explained in the book (maybe by using the index) and check whether you have got it right.
- **Student questions.** This is another way to test and improve your own learning. You should try to answer these questions. Your answers don't count towards your grade for the unit: the questions are to help you learn – not to test you. That's why the section is called build your learning.

It would be a good idea to keep a file of key words and phrases and your answers to student questions, with corrections where necessary, for revision.

How can I learn from work placements?

While you do not have to go on **work experience** to pass your GNVQ qualification, you will learn an enormous amount from a good **work placement**. This is a kind of learning that no amount of book learning or classroom teaching can give you. That's why we have included a short section at the end of the book called 'Work placement in a care setting'.

Making the most of work experience

Read the section in this textbook on work placement in a care setting (pages 232–8). Make a list of five things you intend to learn about when you go on work experience.

How will the book help me to prepare my portfolio?

You have already looked at the assessment evidence you have to produce for Unit 1. This time let's look at the assessment evidence you need to produce for Unit 2. This is set out in the specifications for Unit 2 (ask your tutor for a copy if you do not have one).

Look at the box called 'What you need to produce' – this looks like a lot of work, and it is. However, you have about half a term in which to do it and this book is arranged to help make the job easier. It breaks down the work you have to do into smaller, more reasonably sized, sections. These are called Assessment work and appear throughout each unit. Let's see how this works.

Turn to page 142 of this textbook and look at the grid. This has three columns, the first lists the grade, the second describes the assessment criteria and the third column tells you which tasks you need to do. In this case, you need to do both tasks 1a and 1b to get a pass grade. These tasks are explained in detail under the next heading 'What to do'. When you have done the tasks, you will have satisfied the assessment criteria in the second column of the grid.

In Unit 2, there are further assessment work panels on pages 149 and 156. As you complete the assessment work tasks, you can keep track of your progress by filling in the grid that appears at the end of the unit (see page 159).

If you do all the assessment work tasks as you work through the unit, you should find that you will have completed everything that you need to include in your portfolio of assessment evidence, up to and including the tasks you will need to complete for a distinction. Even if you find Task 3e too difficult (see page 156) but you complete all the others, you will still achieve a merit.

Note that although at the time of publication the assessment work broadly reflects the GNVQ Intermediate Health and Social Care specifications, you should check with your teacher that it matches the most recent specifications.

How should I organise my portfolio?

The last feature in the chapter is called Self-assessment of evidence. This explains how you can organise and present the work in your portfolio as well as possible. You can check whether you have done everything you should have before you hand your work to your tutor for marking.

Answers to external tests (see page ix)

Answers to question 1 might include breast growth, the onset of menstruation and widening of the pelvis. Incorrect answers would be the growth of pubic hair or an increase in height or weight, as these are changes that are also experienced by boys.

Answers to question 2 are physical, because his graze will need to be cleaned and covered with a dressing, and emotional, because falling over and the pain of a grazed knee is likely to have upset him and he will need comforting.

Build your learning

Summary points

- The contents of this book cover all you need to learn for the compulsory units of the GNVQ Intermediate Health and Social Care.

- Activities help you to learn by giving you things to do.

- Case studies help you to think about real situations where care may be needed.

- Build your learning summarises each section, lists key phrases and summary points and asks some questions.

- You will learn a great deal from work experience.

- If you complete all the Assessment work sections and the section called Self-assessment of evidence, you will have all you need for your portfolio.

Key words and phrases

You should know the meaning of the words and phrases listed below as they relate to the organisation of this book. If you're not sure about any of them, go back through the last three pages of this introduction to check and refresh your understanding.

- Preview
- Activities
- Case studies
- Summary points
- Key words and phrases
- Student questions
- Work experience
- Work placement
- Assessment work
- Self-assessment of evidence

Student questions

1 How do activities help you learn?

2 How do case studies help you learn?

3 How does the build your learning section help you learn?

4 Why is work experience important?

5 What do you have to do to complete your portfolio?

Credits

Every effort has been made to contact copyright holders, but if any have been inadvertently overlooked, the publishers will be pleased to make the necessary arrangements at the first opportunity.

The authors and publisher would like to thank the following for permission to reproduce photographs and other material.

Barking Dog Art (pp. 126, 132, 146, 171, 189)

Barnardos (p. 25)

John Birdsall Photography (pp. 30, 183)

Tim Booth (pp. 28, 43, 44, 46, 47, 50 [bottom], 52, 53, 55 [bottom], 87 [centre], 88)

BUPA (p. 26)

Susan Cashin (p.167)

Collections (pp. 31, 166, 218)

Corbis (pp. 9, 170)

DfEE (p. 206)

Sally and Richard Greenhill Photo Library (pp. 45, 187, 233, 136)

Hammersmith and West London College of Further Education (p. 184)

Health Education Authority (pp.102, 103, 112, 113, 121, 124, 130, 134, 145, 150, 151, 152)

Help the Aged (p. 25)

Muriel Kasner (p. 201)

London Borough of Tower Hamlets (p. 64)

Bethan Matthews (pp. 62, 163, 164, 184)

Mother & Baby Picture Library (pp. 1 [top and bottom], 2, 21, 27, 160, 169, 171, 174,175, 178 [except bottom left])

Olga Mundy (p. 220)

National Asthma Campaign (p. 145)

Office for National Statistics (pp. 91, 125, 127, 162)

Photofusion (Vicky White p. 101), (Chrispin Hughes p. 208)

Portman Group (p. 128)

Public Health Laboratory Service (pp. 137, 140)

Joseph Rowntree Foundation (p. 25)

Royal Society for the Prevention of Accidents (p. 136)

Science Photo Library (pp. 4, 123)

Adrian Sutcliffe (pp. 182, 199)

Telegraph Colour Library (p. 131)

Tony Stone Images (pp. 1 [middle], 82, 99, 178 [bottom left], 213)

Typhoo (p. 98)

Kay Wright (pp. 184, 201)

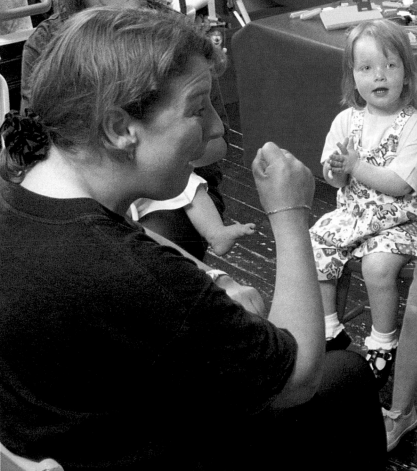

Health, social care and early years provision 1

This unit will help you to develop your knowledge and understanding of the ways in which health, social care and early years education services are provided. You will learn about:

- the main roles of people who work in health, social care and early years services and the structure within which they function

- the value base that underpins all their work with clients

- the skills that they need

- the basic communication skills that they need.

If you are thinking about developing a career in health, social care or early years work you will benefit from a good understanding of the different jobs available and knowledge of the way care services are organised. By learning about the roles of people who already work in these services, and about the entry qualifications, skills and care values that are needed for different kinds of care work, you will be in a better position to make your own career choices and participate in the work of a care team.

The material covers Unit 1, Health, Social Care and Early Years Provision, of the GNVQ Intermediate full award and the GNVQ Intermediate Part One award.

The organisation of health, social care and early years services

You probably know that there are a number of different health, social care and early years organisations in your area. For example, there may be a hospital, health centre or GP practice, nursery or residential home near to where you live. You may have used some of the services that these organisations provide, or perhaps members of your family have used them. Note that not all providers of care will work for large organisations, for example your local dentist, osteopath and childminder are all likely to be self-employed private practitioners.

When we think about providers of care, it's important not to forget that members of our family, our friends and neighbours are also providers of care. A person's parents, partner or close friends are often their first source of care and an ongoing source of care provision. Together these people are referred to as informal carers. We need to include them in our attempt to understand the whole, national system of care.

▶ Care workers

This unit is about all of these kinds of local care providers and the work that they do, but it's also about the whole national system of care provision. The national system of care provision is complex. One way of making the system easier to understand is to divide it up into four different sectors. These are the statutory, voluntary, private and informal sectors (see Figure 1.1).

Figure 1.1: The organisation of health, social care and early years services

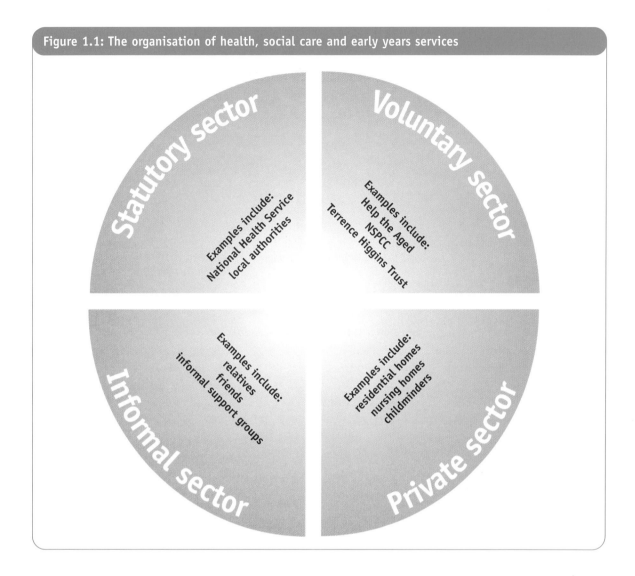

Statutory sector

Examples include:
National Health Service
local authorities

Voluntary sector

Examples include:
Help the Aged
NSPCC
Terrence Higgins Trust

Informal sector

Examples include:
relatives
friends
informal support groups

Private sector

Examples include:
residential homes
nursing homes
childminders

The **statutory sector** is made up of organisations such as National Health Service trusts and local authorities. These organisations deliver the health, social care and early years services which the government has a legal duty to provide. These are known as **statutory services**. The role and organisation of the statutory sector is explained in detail in the next section (see pages 7–24).

The **voluntary sector** is made up of non-governmental organisations, such as MENCAP, a learning disabilities organisation. Voluntary organisations provide many non-statutory services. They don't try to make any financial profit from the services they provide.

The **private sector** is made up of organisations and individual practitioners, such as private nurseries and childminders, who set charges and provide health, social care or early years services for a profit.

The informal sector consists of the very large number of unpaid informal carers who look after members of their own family or friends who have care needs.

The voluntary, private and informal sectors are collectively known as the non-statutory sector. The activities of organisations working in the non-statutory sector are explained in more detail later in this unit (see pages 25–31).

Individuals and organisations in each of the four care sectors make an important contribution to the overall provision of care in the United Kingdom. There are important differences in the type of service that individuals and organisations in the different sectors provide. There are also many areas in which they collaborate and work together.

Build your learning

Summary points

- In the United Kingdom, health, social care and early years services are provided by a number of different kinds of care provider.

- Care services are provided by care organisations, individual private practitioners and informal carers.

- Care providers are said to belong to either the statutory, private, voluntary or informal sectors.

- A statutory organisation is created by law, and is funded and run by the government.

- Informal carers are friends, relatives and neighbours who become involved in providing care for a person in need.

Key words and phrases

You should know the meaning of the words and phrases listed below as they relate to the different types of care organisation and sectors of care. If you are not sure about any of them, go back through the last three pages to check and refresh your understanding.

- **Statutory sector**
- **Voluntary sector**
- **Informal sector**
- **Private sector**
- **Statutory services**
- **Private practitioner**
- **Informal carers**

Student questions

1 How many care sectors are there in the United Kingdom?

2 What are the different care sectors called?

3 Which sector covers the care given by relatives, friends and neighbours?

4 Name two organisations that are part of the statutory sector.

5 Give an example of a private practitioner who works in your area.

The statutory care system

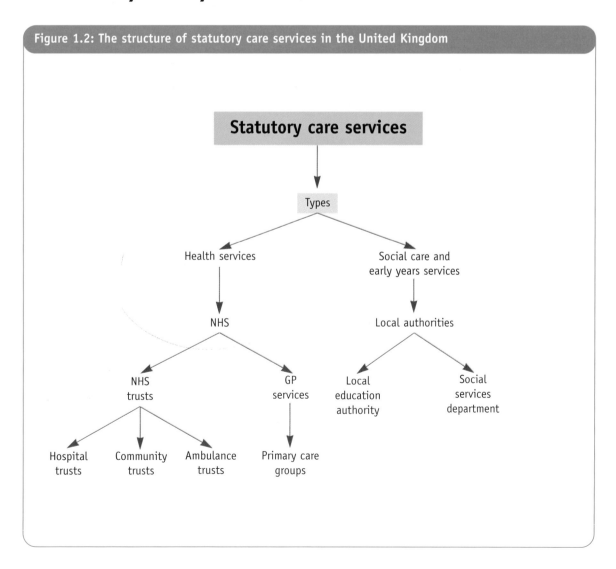

Figure 1.2: The structure of statutory care services in the United Kingdom

Certain health, social care and early years services must, by law, be provided by the government. These are known as **statutory services**. The **statutory sector** includes National Health Service (NHS) and local authority (council) services. Examples of statutory services include free emergency health care and schooling up to the age of sixteen. The statutory system, as we know it today, began in 1948 when the government took on responsibility for providing care services and embarked on the development of the welfare state.

The structure of statutory care and early years services in the United Kingdom is best understood by looking separately at the organisation of health care, social care and early years services (see Figure 1.2).

Statutory health care services

Statutory health care services aim to assess and treat people of all ages who are physically unwell or who have psychological problems. Most of us will have some contact with the statutory health care services at some point in our lives, either for emergency care or more usually because of less severe illness. The first contact that we have will usually be with local-level primary care services, like our GP.

The statutory health service is organised into several levels:

- the national level
- the regional level
- the district level
- the local area level.

The national level

The **Department of Health** is the main government department responsible for statutory health and social care services. The department itself does not provide care services directly and is not responsible for the payment of welfare benefits. The **Department of Social Security** has responsibility for the payment of welfare benefits.

At the national level, politicians and civil servants attached to the Department of Health make decisions about how health care services should be organised and paid for throughout the country. These people, and the department that they work in, are sometimes referred to as **central government**. The politician who has overall responsibility for health care provision is called the **Secretary of State for Health**.

Central government has been the main provider of finance for statutory health, social care and early years services for many years. The money that it provides is used to employ

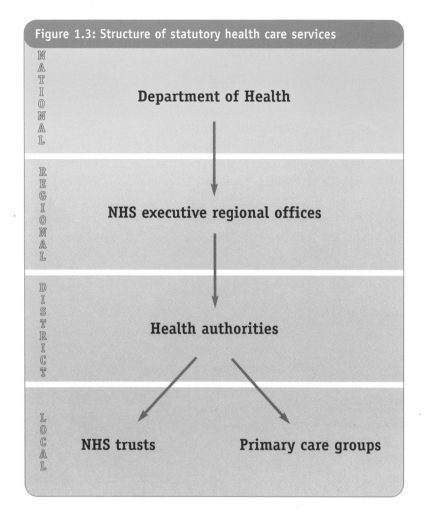

Figure 1.3: Structure of statutory health care services

NATIONAL

Department of Health

REGIONAL

NHS executive regional offices

DISTRICT

Health authorities

LOCAL

NHS trusts   **Primary care groups**

thousands of people in a wide variety of jobs. It funds most hospitals, social service departments and state schools.

The regional level

The next tier in the health care structure is the regional level. England is divided into eight **regional health authorities**. Each of the eight regions has its own **NHS regional executive office** that oversees the funding and running of statutory health care services in its region. Wales, Scotland and Northern Ireland are separate, single country regions and have their own NHS executive offices. The name and location of each of the English regions is shown in Figure 1.4.

The district level

Below the regional health authorities at the district level are **health authorities**. These bodies are responsible for working with local-level organisations to develop a health improvement programme for their district and for making funding agreements to ensure the provision of services that will meet the health care needs of the local population.

Figure 1.4: National Health Service regions in England

The local area level

Health care is delivered at the local level. **NHS trusts** provide hospital and community-based services for a wide range of clients. General practitioners (GPs), dentists, and opticians also provide statutory health care services in locally based practices. All the GPs and community nurses in an area are represented by a **primary care group**. This group takes responsibility for **commissioning** (ordering/requesting) primary health care services for people who live in its area.

Health services provided in the statutory sector

The NHS is the main provider of statutory health care in the United Kingdom. The three main types of care offered to patients in the statutory system are:

- primary health care
- secondary health care
- tertiary health care.

Primary health care

Primary health care organisations are usually the first point of contact for people who need health care. Primary health care is carried out in community settings, such as health centres and clinics, and is provided by a number of practitioners working together as a primary health care team (PHCT). The general practitioner (GP) is a key member of the team. Other primary health care workers include district nurses, community psychiatric nurses and health visitors.

Primary health care workers provide direct care services for the local population. They make home visits to patients who are unable to go to a surgery or health centre. Team members meet regularly to discuss the patients they have in common in order to coordinate their work and make sure that the patient receives the best possible treatment. The GP is often the practitioner who has the responsibility of being the team leader or coordinator.

The PHCT is also involved in providing care in cases of minor illness or injury and in monitoring people's health to prevent them from becoming ill or to prevent their condition worsening. PHCT workers often provide a range of checkups, clinics and classes aimed at health improvement and illness prevention. These are usually publicised in leaflets and posters at health centres and surgeries. Common examples of these health improvement services include weight-loss clinics and smoking and stress-reduction classes.

In many health centres the GP or practice nurse will see people who come in feeling unwell, wanting a diagnosis of their illness and some treatment. Many of these visits are for common complaints like colds, flu, cuts and bruises and psychological problems such as depression and anxiety. If a patient has a more serious illness or requires an operation, a member of the PHCT will refer them to local secondary level services, such as a general hospital.

The PHCT works with the full range of client groups in its area. Team members see babies and young children, teenagers and adults and the elderly and infirm. Most PHCTs run special clinics to meet the varying needs of these groups. The following case study gives you some idea of the range of services that are provided.

CASE STUDY

Working at the health centre

Waverton Health Centre is situated in the centre of Waverton. It is one of three health centres that provide primary health care for the local population. The health centre opens at 7.30 a.m., with an early morning clinic for people who are unable to come during working hours.

The two GPs at the centre, Dr John Cassidy and Dr Richard Kirk, take it in turns to run the early clinic. They see people who are suffering from common, minor complaints, such as colds, flu, sports injuries and illnesses that affect their ability to go to work. Most of the other staff arrive at 8.30 a.m. to prepare for a 9 o'clock start. Arlene Thomas is employed by Dr Cassidy and Dr Kirk as the **practice nurse**. She sees patients for health checks, gives inoculations, carries out cervical smears and is available to see any patient who would rather see a nurse than a GP. Muriel Jones has worked as the **receptionist** for the last five years. She books appointments, greets patients on arrival and looks after patients' medical files. Caroline Evans is the **health visitor** attached to the centre. She sees mothers and babies by appointment in their homes. Caroline also runs health education classes and antenatal clinics at the centre. Raj Ramana is the **community psychiatric nurse** attached to the practice. He sees clients for counselling and gives medication to people who need it to stabilise their mental state. Raj visits patients in their own homes when they are mentally distressed and cannot or do not wish to come to the health centre. The other members of the primary

health care team based at the health centre are **district nurses** Priti Shah and Yvonne Black. Priti and Yvonne usually visit people in their homes to provide care and advise on treatment. Their main area of work is with elderly and physically infirm patients registered at the health centre.

All members of the primary health care team meet each day at 8.30 a.m. to discuss new referrals, patients that they have in common and to plan the work of the day. Sometimes team members decide to work together with a particular patient, but most of the time they see patients indiviudally, referring to each other when specialist help is needed. The team tries to meet all of the primary health care needs of the patients registered with the Waverton Health Centre.

ACTIVITY

Working at the health centre

Try to answer the following questions about Waverton Health Centre.

1 Make a list of all of the health care problems that are dealt with by the staff at Waverton Health Centre.

2 Why do you think some people might prefer to see Arlene Thomas, the practice nurse, rather than a GP at the health centre?

3 Caroline Evans, the health visitor, runs antenatal clinics at the health centre. What are antenatal clinics?

4 Using the information in the case study, what would you say are the main differences between the role of a district nurse and the role of a health visitor?

Secondary health care

Hospitals generally provide a secondary level of health care. They become involved when someone has already been diagnosed with an illness, disease or other condition (such as pregnancy) that requires medical, nursing or other therapeutic

◀ NHS trust hospital

help. Patients who go into hospital have usually been referred to the secondary services of a medical team or a specialist by their GP or by another member of the PHCT. Most secondary hospital care is provided by **NHS trusts**. These are government-funded organisations that have a statutory responsibility to provide health care services. These secondary health care services are provided through a number of different kinds of hospital.

- **District general hospitals** provide a wide range of health care services for the whole population of an area. They provide services for acutely ill people who need an operation or treatment that involves contact with specially trained doctors and nurses.
- **Local community hospitals** usually provide a more limited range of treatments for smaller populations of people in an area. They often have facilities for people to be seen on an outpatient basis and usually have much smaller inpatient facilities than the district general hospital.
- **National teaching hospitals** and **specialist units** provide highly specialist medical, surgical and psychiatric treatments to patients who may be referred from anywhere in the country. Their expertise is available both to inpatients and outpatients. Two examples of this kind of hospital are Great Ormond Street Hospital for Sick Children in London and the Royal National Orthopaedic Hospital at Stanmore, Middlesex.

Tertiary health care

Tertiary health care refers to long-term and rehabilitative care. Tertiary health care is concerned with helping people to adapt and come to terms with an illness or disability that they may have for the rest of their lives. Some tertiary health care, such as long-term physiotherapy, may result in improved functioning and well-being for the patient, depending on the problems that he or she has. Other forms of tertiary care, such as the care offered by hospices, are focused on maintaining the patient's comfort and dignity when his or her condition will result in death. Tertiary care is usually specialist and requires a referral from secondary care providers. The number of people receiving tertiary care is relatively small compared to those receiving primary and secondary care.

The statutory social care system

Social care services are provided to help people who are vulnerable because their age (children or older people) or a disability or impairment (mental illness, physical, sensory or learning disability) means that they are unable to meet aspects of their personal and social needs independently. Social services departments run by local authorities, or councils, have responsibility for statutory social care services.

Two important statutes, or laws, affect the way in which social services departments work:

- the NHS and Community Care Act 1990
- the Children Act 1989.

The NHS and Community Care Act 1990 divided most social services departments into purchasing and providing sections. The purchasing section is involved in buying care services for adult clients whose social care needs have been assessed, and in putting together care packages for them. The provider section delivers some of these services, especially social work. Social services departments pay other voluntary and private sector organisations to provide a lot of the statutory social care services that their adult clients receive.

The Children Act 1989 is the main law influencing statutory social care services for children. This law places a responsibility on social services departments to safeguard and promote the welfare of children in need. For example, social services departments must provide child protection services, services for children under five and somewhere to live for children who are unable to live with their families.

There are two main levels of service organisation in the statutory social care system, the national level and the local level. There are no regional organisations responsible for statutory social care services.

The national level

The top tier is the central government level. This is where the Secretary of State for Health, his or her ministers and the Department of Health civil servants work to make policy and provide the funding for social care services. The Social Care Group of the Department of Health includes the Social Services Inspectorate (SSI). The chief functions of the SSI are to issue guidance to local authorities about social care and also to monitor and inspect their performance.

The local area level

Statutory social care, education and social work services are provided at the local level through local authorities. Local authorities are also known as councils. In rural areas, where the population is relatively small, a county council is usually responsible for providing education and social services. In more

Figure 1.5: Organisation of social services provision

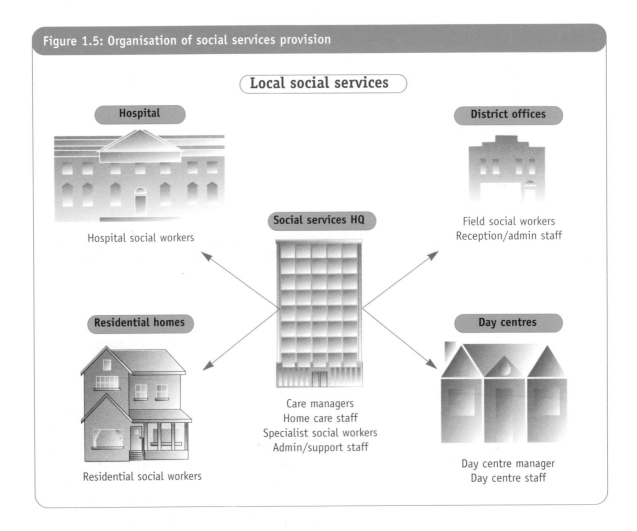

Local social services

Hospital
Hospital social workers

District offices
Field social workers
Reception/admin staff

Social services HQ
Care managers
Home care staff
Specialist social workers
Admin/support staff

Residential homes
Residential social workers

Day centres
Day centre manager
Day centre staff

populated urban areas unitary and borough councils are responsible for provision. All local authorities must have a social services committee, which is made up of local councillors. This committee is responsible for monitoring social services in its area and appoints a director of social services to run the social services department. It is through this department that social care services are provided to the public.

The provider section of the social services department is generally organised into specialist teams according to which service user group they provide for. A specialist team is made up of a group of field social workers who provide social work services to people with particular needs (mental health problems, learning disability, sensory impairments) or who meet particular age criteria (children and families, older people). Some local authority social workers are also employed to work in hospitals and residential homes or take on very specialist roles as, for example, adoption social workers or young offender specialists.

The purchasing section of the social services department is staffed by, amongst others, **care managers** and **care coordinators** who buy, or commission, packages of care for service users and then monitor the way in which they are being delivered. Local authority social services departments also depend on indirect care workers to keep the organisation running. They employ a variety of administrative, managerial and support staff to ensure that the whole organisation is able to function effectively and support the staff who provide direct social care to clients.

CASE STUDY

Working in the Central Area team office

The Central Area team social services office combines several specialist teams for the town of Waverton. There are several teams located in the one building.

The teams located in the main building are:

- the older people and people with disabilities team
- the occupational therapy unit
- the community resource team for older people with mental infirmity
- the home care service.

All the teams share the same **receptionist** Tracey Dunn, whose job is to put callers through to the correct team.

The working day starts at 8.45 a.m. Part of Tracey's job is to distribute the mail to the different teams. A lot of the letters are referrals from other professionals. More and more these days, professionals such as GPs and hospital doctors are choosing to fax their referrals. Tracey's job is to ensure that these get passed on to the right people.

The older people and people with disabilities team consists of 12 social workers, or **care**

coordinators as they are more commonly known. There are four secretarial and administrative staff under Joyce James, the **office manager**. She ensures that the system of case files is run properly, that word processing is completed and that the finances and accounts are sorted out.

Baldish Sahota is the **team manager**. She manages and supervises the care coordinators in their work. Each day two of them are on duty to take telephone enquiries and deal with callers to the office. Paul Harrison is one of the coordinators on duty today. The phones generally get very busy at 9 a.m. with calls from GPs, district nurses, wardens of sheltered housing and members of the public. Paul's job is to clarify details, establish eligibility and make referrals to the care coordinators.

At 9.15 a.m. a district nurse makes an urgent referral. An 85-year-old woman who suffers badly from arthritis and who lives alone has 'gone off her legs' and needs help with meals and personal care three times a day. Paul takes the details and informs Baldish. Baldish knows that she must get one of the care coordinators to go out and complete a needs-led assessment that morning so that a care plan can be put in place later that day. Lynette Cracknell arranges to make a joint visit with the district nurse later that morning.

Lynette decides that she will need to commission some home care and organise a meals service in order to help the woman remain at home. Lynette can commission the home care from a choice of providers. She can use several accredited private home care agencies and the home care service run by social services. On this occasion she decides to commission the care from the social services home care service. She rings the home care manager to request three 30-minute visits a day from a home care assistant. The assistant's job will be to help the elderly woman with personal care such as washing and toileting.

Lynette also feels that, as the elderly woman will continue to have problems with her arthritis, she will benefit from an assessment by an occupational therapist. When she gets back to the office she makes a referral to the occupational therapy team. Lyn Butler, the senior occupational therapist, cannot allocate one of her team immediately, but assures Lynette that the referral will be dealt with as soon as possible.

Back in the team office, Paul is receiving information from the concerned neighbour of a 68-year-old man who was found wandering in the street late last night, obviously confused and at risk. One of Paul's first tasks is to establish whether the man is known to the community resource team. If not, Paul will try to contact the man's GP. As it turns out, the man is known to one of the community resource team's community psychiatric nurses, Mark Goater. Mark will arrange to visit the man to see what the problem is.

As the day continues, Paul and his colleagues respond to various urgent and non-urgent referrals for social care. The other care coordinators are either arranging care, completing paperwork, visiting their clients or monitoring how the care is going by speaking to relatives or to other professionals. Sometimes a complex case may require a care coordinator to call a case conference of all interested parties. This illustrates that a lot of care work is multidisciplinary.

ACTIVITY

The Central Area social services team

Try to answer the following questions about Waverton's Central Area social services team.

1 List the different types of role that the care workers who are part of the Central Area team perform.

2 Identify two direct care workers and two indirect care workers who are based in the Central Area team office.

3 What do you think is involved in a needs-led assessment? Come up with some ideas, identifying the kinds of needs that social care workers would deal with.

4 Lynette Cracknell has to commission some home care for an 85-year-old woman. What does this mean?

5 Read through the case study and identify what Paul Harrison, a care coordinator, has to do when he is on the duty team. In your own words, summarise what being on duty involves.

The statutory early years system

Early years provision is the term given to education and childcare services for children under the age of eight. In the United Kingdom, childcare tends to be seen as the responsibility of parents. There is a lot of informal early years childcare provision and much less statutory provision than in health care, for example.

▼ Looking after young children

The national level

The **Department for Education and Employment** is currently the key government department responsible for early years services at the top level of the statutory system. Again, this government department does not provide early years services directly. The main role of the **Secretary of State for Education and Employment**, his or her ministers and the department's civil servants is to make policy and provide funds for statutory early years and childcare services.

The local level

There are no regional organisations responsible for statutory early years services and there is only a small amount of **statutory day care** provision at the local level. The body responsible for purchasing early years care is the local authority. Early years care and education services are usually provided through the personal social services and education departments of local authorities. Statutory early years provision is usually limited to families where a child is at risk or where there are family pressures and problems that can be reduced if a mother or other children can be helped by the provision of outside childcare support.

Day care can be provided through playgroups, nurseries, childminders and family centres. Children and families who use these services have care and early years needs that have been assessed by a social worker or other early years professional.

The main statutory, or legal, duties that local authorities face regarding early years services are contained in the **Children Act 1989**. This act says that the local education authority (LEA) and the local social services department must review day care services for children under eight at least every three years, and publish the findings. The Children Act 1989 also requires local authorities to provide day care services for children in need. This includes children with disabilities and children who have health or development problems. Some local authorities provide early years services for other children as well but do not, under the present law, have to do so.

Foster carers are people who look after children who are unable to continue living with their own family or relatives. A child can live with a foster carer for a long or a short period of time, depending on his or her needs. The background of any foster carer has to be carefully checked by a local authority social services department. Foster carers are paid an allowance to look after the children who come to live with them in their home. Foster care services are provided either by a local authority social services department or by a voluntary sector organisation, such as Barnardo's.

Registered childminders are people who look after other people's children in their own home. They are registered with the local authority social services department. The Children Act 1989 made it a requirement that all people who provide a childminder service, and the premises in which they care for the children, must be assessed as suitable by, and be registered with, their local authority. It is the legal responsibility of the social services department to carry out assessments and keep the register. Childminders usually work privately, charging and collecting fees for their services.

CASE STUDY

Working in the Ferry Centre nursery

The Ferry Centre is a day nursery that is run by Waverton social services department. It caters for up to 75 children between the ages of six months and four and a half years.

The nursery facilities include a baby room for children aged six to 18 months, and three other rooms for children age 18 months to two years, two to three years and three to four years. The Ferry Centre has limited places, for which there is a high demand. Children are referred to the nursery by a variety of health, social care and early years education workers. They can only be accepted and offered a place if one or more of the following criteria are met.

- The child's parents are mentally or physically unwell and are unable to care for them without help.

- The child is on the child protection register and requires a safe environment where his or her developmental needs can be met.

- The child has special needs, such as developmental delay.

- The child's parents are experiencing a temporary crisis and need support and assistance with childcare.

The **child protection register** is a list of children whose welfare and safety are felt to be at risk. It is compiled and managed by the local authority social services department. About 80 per cent of the children attending the Ferry Centre nursery are on Waverton's child protection register.

Avis Gardner is the nursery manager. She is a qualified nursery nurse (NNEB) with managerial qualifications and experience. She has overall responsibility for all the children and staff in the nursery and leads the day-to-day management and running of the nursery. Avis has regular supervision and support from her line manager Franklin Jones, who is based at the town hall. Annette Gibson is the receptionist at the Ferry Centre. She takes phone calls and does administrative work, such as typing and filing.

Other staff employed at the nursery include a deputy nursery manager, six qualified nursery nurses, six nursery assistants, two cooks and three part-time cleaners. The nursery nurses act as key workers to individual children. Each key worker has responsibility for planning and monitoring the care and education received by the children in their care. The nursery assistants work with the children and carry out a lot of the care and education activities. Each day is filled with a variety of play and interaction activities designed to promote learning and development for the children.

The Ferry Centre is a very busy nursery. The day starts at 8 a.m., and from this time onwards, children are dropped off by their parents or carers. Avis often begins the day by showing a new child and his or her parents around the nursery. Today she is meeting Joel Young, aged three and a half, who starts nursery on Monday. As this is his first morning, this is only an introductory visit. Joel's parents will be asked to stay for an hour or two so that they can look around the nursery. They will also be encouraged to ask questions and get to know Joel's key worker who will be responsible for him throughout his time at the nursery. They will then be encouraged to leave Joel with the nursery staff for another couple of hours.

Joel's allocated key worker is Monica Mitchell, one of the nursery nurses. She will have direct individual responsibility for his learning programme, will concentrate on promoting conversation and interaction between Joel and the other children, and will monitor his physical and psychological development. Monica will provide regular feedback on Joel's development and progress to his parents. Many children are offered full-time places from Monday to Friday, if their situation warrants it. In other cases the admission is staggered throughout the week. Joel will be attending on Mondays, Wednesdays and Fridays.

Ula Haynes is the allocated child and family social worker for the Young family. Shortly after Joel's parents left, Monica phones Ula to let her know that the visit is going well

and that the family seemed happy with the arrangements made for Joel so far.

The Ferry Centre staff have regular contact with a wide range of health and social care professionals. After meeting Joel Young and his parents, Avis takes a phone call from Abby Byers, a health visitor. Abby is calling to find out about vacancies for one of her clients. A place is urgently required because Sylvester Johnson, a three-year-old, has delayed speech development. Abby informs Avis that she had discussed Sylvester's needs with a speech therapist, who had also assessed him, and would be sending an urgent referral letter that afternoon. As Avis puts the phone down, Aisha George, a dietician, walks into her office. Aisha has come to the nursery to review the menus of six children who are on special diets because they have medical conditions, including diabetes and coeliac disease. She makes minor changes to the planned diets and impresses upon Avis and the cooks at the centre the importance of the children receiving their special diets. During the day, two other professional care workers, an occupational therapist and an audiologist, call Avis to arrange visits to see two of the children. Avis passes the calls to the allocated key workers for the children. Both children have hearing loss and muscular difficulties as a result of mild cerebral palsy.

As you can see, the roles of the staff and the support workers vary considerably in a nursery but basically they are all involved in promoting and protecting the growth, development and welfare of the children in their care.

ACTIVITY

Working at Ferry Centre

Try to answer the following questions about the Ferry Centre nursery.

1 What kind of organisation (statutory, voluntary, private) is the Ferry Centre nursery? Give a reason to support your answer.

2 What is the child protection register and why might a child's name be put on it?

3 What is involved in being a key worker at the Ferry Centre nursery?

4 Why is it a good idea for children and their parents to have a short introductory visit to the nursery? Think about how this would benefit the child, parents and the staff.

5 What feature of the children's ability will the audiologist assess when she visits the nursery?

Build your learning

Key words and phrases

You should know the meaning of the words and phrases listed below that relate to the organisation of health, social care and early years services. If necessary, go back through the last 15 pages to refresh your understanding.

- Department of Health
- Department of Social Security
- Secretary of State for Health
- Department for Education and Employment
- Central government
- Health care services
- NHS Regional Executive
- NHS trust hospital
- Primary health care
- Primary health care team
- Primary care group
- Secondary health care
- Tertiary health care
- Local authority
- Social care services
- Registered childminder
- Local education authority
- Foster carer
- Children Act 1989
- NHS and Community Care Act 1990

Summary points

- There are a number of different levels of organisation in the statutory care system.

- Direct care services are provided by local level organisations.

- The National Health Service is the main provider of statutory health care services in the United Kingdom.

- Local authority social services departments are responsible for statutory social care services throughout the United Kingdom. Health and social service trusts have this responsibility in Northern Ireland.

- Health care services are often organised into primary, secondary and tertiary services.

- Primary health care services are community-based 'first point of contact' services. Secondary health care services are hospital-based services. Tertiary services are specialist hospital services.

- Local authority education and social services departments have responsibility for early years childcare and education services.

 Student questions

1 What are the three different levels of the statutory care system called?

2 Give two examples of local level statutory health care services in your area.

3 Which two central government departments have responsibility for health, social care and early years services?

4 How would you explain the difference between primary and secondary health care?

5 What kind of social care services are local authorities responsible for?

Non-statutory organisations

There are three main types of service provider in the non-statutory sector:

- voluntary sector organisations
- private sector organisations and private practitioners
- informal carers.

Voluntary sector organisations

The voluntary care sector has its origins in the nineteenth century when there were very few statutory care services for ordinary people and when most private services were beyond the financial reach of all but the rich. Charities and voluntary organisations grew out of the donations of a few rich people and the campaigns of philanthropists. These were wealthy individuals, such as Joseph Rowntree, who wished to help their local communities and reduce the deprivation and suffering that they saw around them.

The voluntary sector now includes large organisations that work throughout the United Kingdom, as well as very small groups that work for a cause in their local area. National

▼ Joseph Rowntree

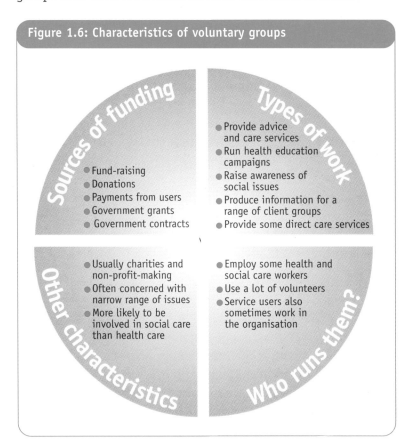

Figure 1.6: Characteristics of voluntary groups

Sources of funding
- Fund-raising
- Donations
- Payments from users
- Government grants
- Government contracts

Types of work
- Provide advice and care services
- Run health education campaigns
- Raise awareness of social issues
- Produce information for a range of client groups
- Provide some direct care services

Other characteristics
- Usually charities and non-profit-making
- Often concerned with narrow range of issues
- More likely to be involved in social care than health care

Who runs them?
- Employ some health and social care workers
- Use a lot of volunteers
- Service users also sometimes work in the organisation

▲ Two care organisations within the voluntary sector

voluntary organisations include MENCAP, which campaigns for people with learning difficulties, Help the Aged, which works on behalf of older people and the National Society for the Prevention of Cruelty to Children (NSPCC).

These big voluntary organisations tend to have many local branches and a national headquarters that coordinates the work of the organisation's branches around the country. The large number of small voluntary groups that exist in the United Kingdom are usually concerned with a very specific or local issue, or provide a service to meet a particular local need. An example might be a support group for single parents or a local playgroup that aims to meet the needs of a group of children with autism.

Most voluntary sector organisations are **registered charities**. This means that they finance their services and the running of their organisation through fund-raising for voluntary donations. They may also receive grants from central or local government, or small payments from service users, but they put their income back into running their services. Voluntary organisations recruit a lot of unpaid **volunteers** who provide their time and skills for free, but they also employ some care workers, managers and administrative staff as paid employees.

Private sector organisations

Private companies, independent practitioners and self-employed carers have a long tradition of providing both health and social care to people who are able to pay for their services. Private sector organisations charge their clients fees in order to make a profit for their shareholders. Independent, self-employed practitioners also provide private services and charge fees in order to make a living for themselves.

The private sector offers a narrower range of services and has fewer organisations and clients than either the statutory or voluntary sectors. Within the private sector there are a lot more health care and early years organisations than social care organisations. Many of the services that are provided in the private sector cannot be obtained in the statutory system and are specialist, non-emergency services.

Health care

Private sector health care organisations include a number of large companies, such as BUPA and Nuffield Hospitals, which provide complex health care services, including surgery, in their own private hospitals. It is also possible to receive health care as a private patient in a ward or unit of an NHS trust hospital

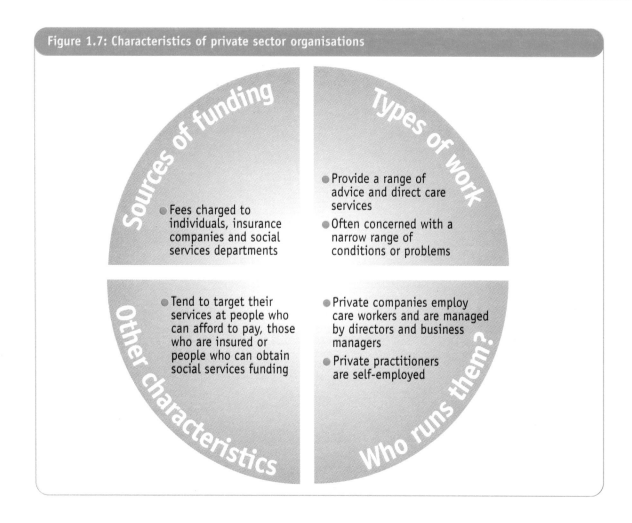

Figure 1.7: Characteristics of private sector organisations

Sources of funding
- Fees charged to individuals, insurance companies and social services departments

Types of work
- Provide a range of advice and direct care services
- Often concerned with a narrow range of conditions or problems

Other characteristics
- Tend to target their services at people who can afford to pay, those who are insured or people who can obtain social services funding

Who runs them?
- Private companies employ care workers and are managed by directors and business managers
- Private practitioners are self-employed

that is owned or leased by a private company such as BUPA or Nuffield Hospitals. As well as direct care services, such as hospitals, there are now a large number of private sector employment agencies that specialise in recruiting and providing health care staff to other statutory, voluntary and private organisations.

Private sector health care clients often pay the costs of their care through health insurance that they have taken out as a precaution against illness and the need for care at different times of their lives.

Social care
There are relatively few private sector social care organisations. Those that do exist tend to specialise in residential care for older people and people with disabilities and in domiciliary, or home care, services. People who use private sector social care services either have to pay for the cost of the services themselves or, if they meet the criteria, may have their fees paid by their local authority social services department.

Early years

A private nursery

Early years services in the private sector include nursery schools, playgroups, crèches and childminding services. These organisations provide childcare and early years services to young children who have needs that are not met by the limited range of statutory sector services. As a child's parents must be able to afford to pay the fees charged, private sector childcare services are not available to everyone who might need or benefit from them. People who use private sector childcare and early years services usually have to pay the fees directly from their own income.

Self-employed carers and private practitioners

Not all private sector care workers are employed in a company. There is also a significant group of care workers who are self-employed. Health care workers, such as dentists, physiotherapists and opticians, and social care workers such as counsellors and psychotherapists, sometimes offer their services through a private practice. Sometimes these services provide clients with an alternative to those available at the local NHS trust hospital, whilst in other circumstances they offer specialist services that are not available in the statutory or voluntary sector. An example might be osteopathy or acupuncture.

▼ Many dentists are self-employed and work in private practice

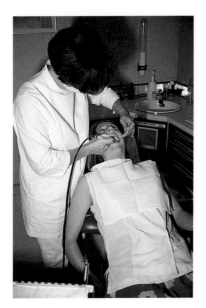

Some carers also work in their own homes on a self-employed basis. Registered childminders are the largest group of self-employed carers working in this way. Like all self-employed carers, they charge the people who use their services a fee for their time and expertise.

Informal carers

Many people who need care and support are not catered for in the formal health care system. Important sources of informal care and support are provided by unpaid, and often untrained, carers such as:

- family members
- friends
- neighbours
- local support groups.

Most of the health and social care for sick and vulnerable people in the United Kingdom is provided by non-professional carers working informally, outside of care organisations. The vast majority of childcare for children under five is also provided in this way. **Informal care** is a broad term that refers to the many ways in which an individual's family, friends and neighbours can provide care and support either without the aid of care professionals or with some assistance from them. Children, the elderly and the long-term sick are the main client groups which benefit from such informal care. The pattern of people caring for their elderly relatives and children at home is well established.

Children also provide informal care (see the article reproduced on page 30). There are a number of different forms of care provided by children when acting as informal carers.

- Informal nursing care involves children giving direct help and practical support to help their relative to meet his or her physical needs. This might include aspects of personal care, such as washing and dressing a parent, or helping him or her to move around when he or she has a mobility problem.
- There are also a wide variety of tasks that children, and informal carers generally, undertake to provide help in the home. Cleaning the house, washing clothes, doing the shopping and cooking are all aspects of informal care that may be a part of a carer's regular routine.
- The third aspect of informal care – companionship – is possibly the most valued but least obvious. Many people who have a disability or illness that limits their ability to care for themselves, and to get out to meet others, value the company and friendship of their carers as much as the practical help they receive.

Children suffer as they care for disabled parents

Children as young as nine are neglecting school work and friends to look after disabled parents at home, according to a study published today. Young carers tend not to draw official attention to their own needs out of fear that the family would be broken up. Their contributions go largely unrecognised and their problems remain invisible until family problems develop into a crisis, the report says.

Sandra Billsborrow, who carried out the research for the Barnardo's children's charity and the Carers' National Association, concludes that a fundamental assessment of the role of young carers is required. Her study combined research over the last decade with interviews on Merseyside with eleven young carers and 45 professionals – mainly doctors, social workers and community nurses.

The young people, mainly females aged between nine and twenty-one, were caring for relatives with disabilities ranging from multiple sclerosis and arthritis to quadriplegia and the aftereffects of strokes. They were asked about their responsibilities, how these affected school and social life, and about their knowledge of parental illness or disability. For some it was the first time they had spo-

ken about looking after the parent. Most felt they could leave the dependent relative for at least a few hours but all said they were concerned about accidents to them while they were away. Some, particularly those who had cared for several years, reported feelings of powerlessness about changing the situation. One 15-year-old said:

'It gets you down and it wears you down. You grow up fast, as well. Sometimes you just want to go out and have a laugh. You can't say, "Right, I've done that for my mum, and she'll be all right tonight." You always have to do something for her. You've never finished the job.'

Most of those sampled had taken days off school because of their domestic responsibilities. Those duties took their toll on friendships, through lack of time for social life. Interviews with professionals suggested the young carers were rarely regarded as recipients of social services – more an essential link in the chain of support provided to the parent. In one case, a home help service was withdrawn from a disabled adult when the sole carer, a teenaged child, was deemed able to cope alone. 'In a climate of limited resources, services are prioritised and, for this reason, the young carer was seen by the home help service as a resource rather than as "in need".'

Judy Jones, *The Independent*, May 1992

The Carers (Recognition and Services) Act 1995 entitles informal carers to an assessment of their needs. The assessment gives the carer the chance to explain how caring affects them and to say what they feel their own needs are, including whether they wish to go on caring for the person whom they look after. The carer's views must be taken into account when social services are arranging care services for the person being looked after. The Carers (Recognition and Services) Act 1995 does give carers the right to an assessment but it doesn't give them the right to receive support services themselves. Often the social workers who conduct the assessment will recommend that the carer receives some extra support but they cannot guarantee that this will be provided.

Informal support groups

Support groups are a second important way in which informal care is provided in the United Kingdom. There are many thousands of local, informal support groups operating throughout the United Kingdom at the present time. They are set up and run by carers and people who have special health and social care needs. The groups may be small and short term, or may have become well established and provide regular, ongoing support to an individual or a group of clients.

The purpose of informal support groups is to provide practical and emotional support to informal carers and the people they care for. An informal support group may consist of neighbours who share childcare arrangements, people in a local area who all look after a relative alone at home, or a group of people who have got together to raise money to help an individual to finance his or her medical or social care needs.

CASE STUDY

Informal care for an elderly person

Mrs Bell is 79 years old and lives alone. She has some memory impairment and forgets what time of the day it is, whether she has eaten, and also the names of all but her closest relatives and her neighbour, Mrs Scott. Mrs Bell is unable to walk any distance due to her arthritis, very rarely goes out alone, and feels frightened of using her bath as she has difficulty getting in and out.

Caring for Mrs Bell

Try to answer the following questions about Mrs Bell.

1 What forms of informal care would Mrs Bell benefit from?

2 Who might be able to provide each form of informal care for Mrs Bell?

3 If you were a relative or neighbour of Mrs Bell's, how would you feel about giving up some of your time to offer Mrs Bell informal care and support?

Build your learning

Summary points

- Voluntary and private sector organisations form what is known as the independent, or non-statutory sector. Both types of organisation are independent from government.

- Voluntary sector organisations are usually registered charities. They can be large, national organisations or very small local groups.

- Voluntary sector organisations obtain a lot of their money through fund-raising and voluntary donations but they are also sometimes funded by social services departments to provide direct social care services.

- Voluntary organisations rely on the help of many unpaid volunteer workers but also employ paid staff.

- Private sector care organisations and self-employed care workers charge people fees to use their services.

- Private care organisations tend to specialise in care services that people are prepared to pay for, such as day care nurseries, residential and nursing homes.

- A lot of care in the United Kingdom is provided by people's relatives and friends who are referred to as informal carers.

Key words and phrases

You should know the meaning of the words and phrases listed below that relate to health, social care and early years services. If you are not sure about any of them, go back through the last eight pages to check and refresh your understanding.

- Registered charity
- Volunteers
- Voluntary organisation

- Private sector
- Private practice
- Self-employed carer

- Informal care
- Informal carer
- Informal support group

Student questions

1 What are the origins of the voluntary sector?

2 Name five care organisations (national or local) that are part of the voluntary sector.

3 Who works in and runs voluntary organisations?

4 How do private sector organisations raise money to fund their care services?

5 What are the main differences between so-called formal and informal carers?

ASSESSMENT WORK

Investigating local care organisations

Health, social care and early years services are provided by organisations throughout the United Kingdom. This activity gives you an opportunity to find out about services provided in two of your local care organisations. The work that you do here will become a part of your end of unit assignment.

	Assessment criteria	Which tasks do I need to do?
Pass	Correctly identify the care sector and client group associated with your chosen organisations.	1a 1b 1c

If you carry out the following activities now, you will have completed part of the work needed for your end of unit assignment.

What to do

1a Identify and name two local care organisations and briefly describe examples of the services that they offer.

1b Identify which care sector each organisation belongs to. Explain the reasons for your decisions.

1c Identify and describe the client group(s) that each organisation's services are aimed at.

You should base your work on two different local care organisations that you can arrange access to. You may also want to complete the assessment work activity on page 58 about the role of local care workers when you visit your chosen organisations.

The main jobs in health, social care and early years services

The NHS is the largest employer in Europe. Within the statutory health and social care sectors in the United Kingdom it is estimated that there are more than a million people in paid employment. There is also an extremely large number of people providing care in the childcare and early years sector. In this part of the unit we will look at the range of jobs in health and social care, identify the main job types and look at what is actually involved in training and working as a health, social care or early years worker.

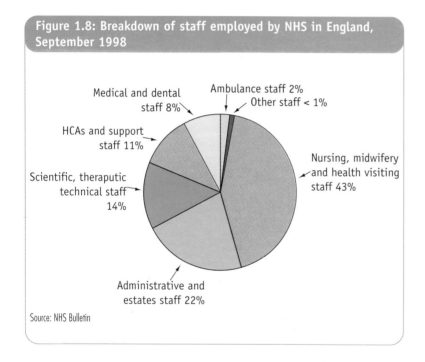

Figure 1.8: Breakdown of staff employed by NHS in England, September 1998

Medical and dental staff 8%

Ambulance staff 2%

Other staff < 1%

HCAs and support staff 11%

Scientific, theraputic technical staff 14%

Nursing, midwifery and health visiting staff 43%

Administrative and estates staff 22%

Source: NHS Bulletin

There is a wide variety of different jobs and specialist roles in health, social care and early years workplaces. Many of these roles are complementary, as care workers often work in teams and coordinate their efforts to help service users. In order to simplify the range of care roles it is useful to consider the differences between:

- health care, social care and early years roles
- direct care workers and support service workers.

Health, social care and early years roles

People employed as health care workers usually deal with individuals of all ages who have physical, medical-related problems such as a disease, injury or acute illness. **Social care workers** usually deal with clients who are vulnerable and who have care needs that are mainly social, emotional or financial rather than medical in nature. **Early years workers** are usually employed in childcare and early years education services for children under the age of eight.

Many clients have both health and social care problems. This means that health care workers may need to provide social care as part of their support of a client. For example, a community psychiatric nurse may need to offer both health and social care.

ACTIVITY

Health, social care or early years?

Look at the following list of health and social care jobs. Reorganise them into three lists headed health jobs, social care jobs and early years roles.

- District nurse
- Community psychiatric nurse
- Care manager
- Social worker
- Nursery nurse
- Housing advice worker
- Health visitor
- Residential social worker
- Hospital manager
- Gynaecologist
- Chiropodist
- Home care assistant
- Childminder
- Hostel manager
- Surgeon

Write a sentence that briefly describes what you believe is involved in each job. You could use careers booklets and computer databases to find out about occupational roles.

Direct care workers and support service workers

People who work in health, social care and early years services may be involved in direct or indirect care roles. **Direct care** involves caring for clients. Examples of people who work in direct care include nursery nurses and occupational therapists. **Indirect care** involves providing support services. For example, people who work in hospital laboratories, catering staff, porters or security staff have indirect care roles in health organisations. Social services departments employ care coordinators whose job is to assess and arrange care for clients but they don't actually carry out the care tasks themselves. In all hospitals, social services departments, nurseries, schools and health centres some workers care directly for service users while others run the organisation and support the direct carers.

Direct care workers such as doctors, nurses and social workers are the people we are most likely to remember coming into contact with. We are less likely to notice the support and indirect care workers who operate behind the scenes. Figure 1.9 shows how a hospital consists of people operating in these two types of role.

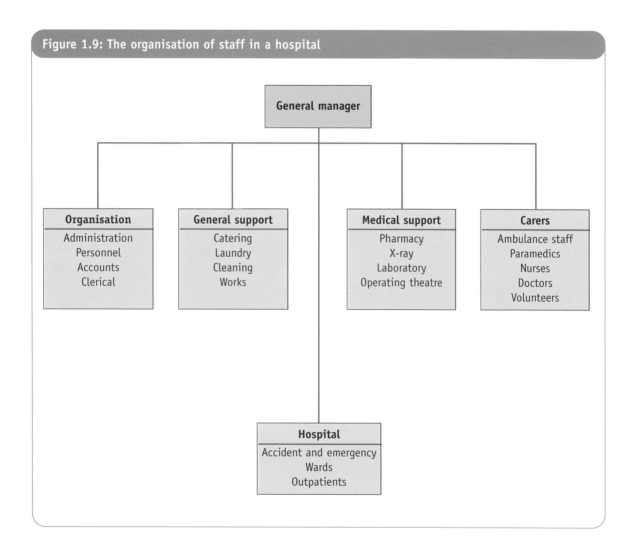

Figure 1.9: The organisation of staff in a hospital

Occupational areas in health and social care

So far we have identified the differences between health care, social care and early years jobs (with some overlaps) and direct care and support roles. Jobs in health and social care can also be grouped into occupational areas. Some of the more familiar occupational areas are:

- medicine
- nursing
- social work
- social care
- childcare
- early years education
- professions allied to medicine (PAMs)
- administration and support work.

Within each of these occupational areas there are many specialist roles that develop after core occupational training has been undertaken. For example, within childcare a person could begin his or her career as a nursery assistant, then qualify and work as a nursery nurse and, with further experience and training, go on to become a classroom teacher in primary education, or a nursery manager for a local authority. Care workers tend to undertake a general training in one of the occupational areas to gain their basic qualification and then specialise in a particular area of that occupation.

Preparing for work in health, social care and early years services

Most students who choose a GNVQ Intermediate Health and Social Care course have made a decision that they would like to work in an area of the care services. Some students make decisions early on about which specific roles and areas of work they are interested in, while others take longer to decide.

If you are in either of these groups, there are three main areas to research and think through before you arrive at a final decision. These are the:

- personal qualities and experience needed for a particular role
- minimum age and qualification requirements
- possible ways in which your career might develop in a particular area.

Careful thinking and preparation in the early stages of your career in care work will help you to achieve what you want later on.

Personal qualities and experience

Care work is all about working with other people, often at times in their lives when they are vulnerable and distressed. To be able to do this, care workers must have a strong sense of wanting to help others and the ability to work with a wide

variety of people. Many students choosing courses such as
GNVQ Intermediate Health and Social Care feel that they have a
caring personality and that they possess the right qualities
needed to care for others.

Would I make a good carer?

1 Brainstorm a list of qualities that you associate with a
'good carer'.

2 Swap ideas with a partner and try to explain to him or
her the importance of each item in your list.

3 Discuss which of these qualities you currently possess
and which you feel you need to develop further.

In order to gain entry to jobs and training courses in care
work, it is often necessary to show that you are able to use
your caring qualities in practical ways. Gaining experience of
care work is important to test out for yourself whether the
practical aspects of care jobs match up to your expectations of
them. Building up your experience is an important way of
demonstrating to employers and course tutors that you are
suitable and committed to a career in this area.

As part of your GNVQ Intermediate Health and Social Care
course you may gain basic experience of care work through
work placements (see page 233 for more information). You may
also have, or be able to gain, experience through providing
informal care to relatives, friends or neighbours. Experience
gained through part-time, full-time and temporary work is
valuable in supporting your learning in school or college and
will help you to progress further.

Qualification requirements

Education and training are just as important as experience in
enabling you to develop effective skills and the values needed
to work in all areas of health, social care and early years
services.

There are currently three different qualification routes into
care work for young people and adults. These are shown in
Figure 1.10.

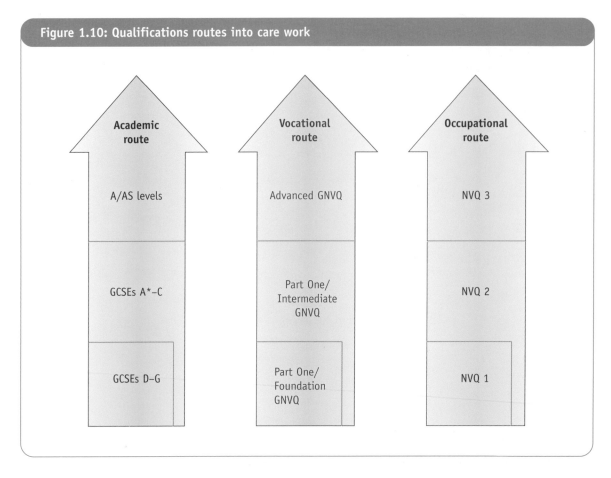

Figure 1.10: Qualifications routes into care work

Some areas of care work, particularly medicine, occupational therapy, and physiotherapy require students to follow the **academic route** into higher education. People who choose this route have to achieve a degree-level qualification. There is a variety of higher education courses available for potential care workers but only a relatively small number of people take this route into care work compared to the GNVQ and NVQ routes.

Health and Social Care GNVQ qualifications provide a school or college-based vocational route that can also lead to higher education or enable students to progress to employment. These qualifications are particularly aimed at 16–19 year old students with little experience in care work who wish to have both employment and further study options. The courses give students a broad underpinning knowledge of the care area and help them to improve their core communication, application of number, and information technology skills. Students can progress from GNVQ Intermediate Health and Social Care courses into a variety of support work or nursery, classroom and care assistant posts.

NVQs are qualifications gained on the job. The **work-based NVQ route** is used to improve the skills and career prospects of people who wish to have a practical role in a health, social care or early years service. People usually begin NVQ courses by either getting a paid job with a care organisation or a training place with their local training and enterprise council (TEC) or college of further education. NVQs cover a variety of areas of adult and childcare work and enable students to establish and improve practical skills.

Build your learning

Summary points

- A large number of people are employed in a broad variety of direct and indirect care roles in health, social care and early years organisations in the United Kingdom.

- Health care roles involve working with people who are physically or mentally unwell.

- Social care roles involve working with people who have personal, social or financial problems.

- Early years workers work with children under eight.

- Direct care usually means hands-on or face-to-face work with patients or clients.

- Indirect care roles are usually support roles, like administration or clerical work.

- Appropriate qualifications, personal qualities and practical experience are all needed by people who wish to gain a professional care qualification.

Key words and phrases

You should know the meaning of the words and phrases listed below that relate to types of jobs in, and ways of training for, health, social care and early years work. If you are not sure about any of them, go back through the last seven pages to check and refresh your understanding.

- **Health care worker**
- **Social care worker**
- **Early years worker**
- **Direct care**
- **Indirect care**
- **Vocational qualifications**
- **Academic qualifications**
- **Occupational areas**
- **Work-based qualifications**
- **NVQs**

Student questions

1 Which is the largest group of care workers in the United Kingdom?

2 How would you explain the difference between what a health care worker and a social care worker does?

3 What is the difference between a direct and an indirect care role?

4 What kind of indirect care roles are performed by people working in hospitals? Name at least three.

5 What type of qualifications can be gained through learning and practising in the workplace?

Career routes and training

In this section we look at the career routes that people may follow to get into and develop careers in each of the different occupational areas. When you are thinking about how you might develop your career in a particular care role it is important to compare the popular image – the stereotype – of the role with the reality. Often the real work patterns, conditions and responsibilities that care workers experience are very different to those portrayed on television and in newspapers and magazines. In reality, care work is much less glamorous than some television programmes suggest!

Medicine

To qualify as a doctor it is necessary to get a degree in medicine. This involves attending a university medical school for five years to gain the basic academic knowledge and practical experience to pass this first stage of medical training. To gain entry to medical school an applicant needs at least five GCSEs and three A levels with high grades. Most students enter medical school at the age of 18.

When a person qualifies at university, he or she must then work for at least a year as a **junior house officer** in a hospital setting, rapidly gaining experience of a range of diseases, illnesses and medical problems. Following this, junior doctors undertake further professional examinations to become specialists in an area of medical practice, such as surgery, general practice or psychiatry.

Doctors must continually update their knowledge through reading specialist journals that cover the latest research, and by attending courses to develop and improve their skills. Hospital doctors gradually work their way up the career ladder from house officer to registrar, then to senior registrar and finally consultant. GPs take a specialist training course after gaining basic hospital experience.

Doctors often work long hours and may work at weekends, in the evenings and at night to deal with the very large caseloads of patients they must see and treat. It can take doctors many years to progress up the career ladder and, while they do this, they are required to continue studying and working.

CASE STUDY

The anaesthetist

Dr Sandra Saunders has worked as an anaesthetist at St Joseph's hospital for the last three years. She works a shift rotation system, which means that, together with her six colleagues in the anaesthetics department, she works shifts to cover the 24-hour needs of the hospital and its patients. She works in the accident and emergency department and in the hospital's operating theatres. Her job is to anaesthetise patients and then to manage their airway and respiratory system safely while they are being treated or operated on. Dr Saunders works closely with other doctors and nursing staff as part of the team on call. As a senior anaesthetist, she attends regular meetings with hospital managers to represent her colleagues and department on the hospital management committee.

CASE STUDY

The general practitioner

Dr Natasha Olabogun works as a GP in an inner-city health centre with three other GPs. After medical school, and two years as a hospital doctor, she took a specialist GP training course. She now has a large and varied list of patients and sees them by appointment and at drop-in clinics between 8.30 a.m. and 6 p.m. each weekday. Dr Olabogun is able to diagnose and treat most of the illnesses that her patients come to her with, but she refers more complicated and serious cases to the local hospital. Dr Olabogun and her colleagues take it in turns to be on call one weekend in every four.

Nursing

Nurses make up the largest group of care staff in the United Kingdom. There are approximately 345,000 qualified nurses working in a range of areas of health care. There are important differences in the type of training and work that professionally qualified nurses and vocationally qualified health care support workers (also known as nursing assistants) undertake.

Registered nursing

To become a professionally qualified nurse, a person must undertake an approved nurse training programme that lasts for three years and results in a registered nurse qualification. The minimum entry qualifications are passes in five GCSEs or equivalent. The minimum age for entry to nurse training is 17 and a half. Since the introduction of the Project 2000 training programme, all applicants undertake an 18-month common foundation course in basic physical and social sciences and nursing studies. They can then choose to specialise in adult, mental health, learning disabilities or children's nursing in the final 18 months of their course.

When qualified, a registered nurse generally works as a staff nurse to gain experience and improve his or her practical skills. Registered nurses work a variety of shift patterns, including days, nights and sometimes weekends. They must update their knowledge and skills continuously through attendance on courses, through personal study and by reading about the latest research and practice in professional magazines and journals. Many registered nurses choose to undertake further specialist courses to progress in their careers.

Nursing is often a physically and emotionally tiring job. Caring for people who are sick and dependent can involve carrying out tasks that are unpleasant and physically demanding, such as changing and remaking soiled beds. As well as carrying out their care role, nurses have to complete administrative work relating to patients and often have a role in training student nurses.

CASE STUDY

The unit manager

Kate Seaman is unit manager for a children's surgical unit in a major teaching hospital. After qualifying as a registered general nurse fifteen years ago, she worked her way up to become ward sister of a surgical ward. She has also worked in operating theatres and gained her BSc degree in nursing five years ago. Kate developed an interest in management and took some short courses to support her practical skills in this area. Two years ago she became unit manager for the surgical unit where she had worked as a sister. Kate would like to spend more time as a manager and intends to undertake a teaching course so that she can pass on her skills and experience to others.

CASE STUDY

The registered general nurse

Marjorie Manzoma qualified as a registered general nurse ten years ago. After gaining some experience as a staff nurse in a hospital medical ward, she undertook further training in psychiatric nursing. Marjorie now combines her general and mental health nursing experience by working in a unit for frail elderly people who experience confusion and memory problems. Marjorie would like to continue working with this group and plans to increase her skills and experience through working in a day care centre and then as a community psychiatric nurse.

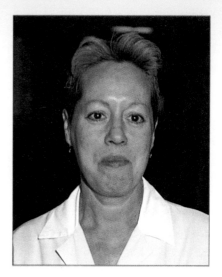

Health care support workers

The other way in which people can gain some vocational training and experience in nursing is as a health care support worker. Most health care support workers follow the NVQ route and gain their training and experience under the supervision of registered nurses. Health care support workers are increasingly trained and qualified to NVQ level 2 or 3 and may be found working in all areas of health care. They often have a great deal of direct patient contact, assisting registered nurses and other care staff in providing care.

The role of a health care support worker is different to that of a registered nurse in a number of important ways.

- Health care support workers carry out most of the domestic tasks in a care setting, such as making beds.
- The physical care that health care support workers provide relates to routine procedures such as lifting, bathing and dressing patients.
- Health care support workers carry out care planned by registered nurses.`

Like nurses, health care support workers work both day and night shift patterns and may also work weekends. There is no minimum age requirement for health care support workers. Personal maturity is one of the key factors that employers take into account when recruiting people to support worker posts.

CASE STUDY

The health care support worker

Stephen Wilkes is 22 years old. He has worked as a health care support worker in a learning disabilities unit for the last five years. He works day and night shifts and provides direct care and support for the ten residents of the bungalow where he works. Stephen helps the residents in different ways depending on their individual needs. Some people need help with personal care, such as going to the toilet, washing and dressing, others need assistance when travelling to college or on social outings. All of the residents benefit from the relationships that they have developed with Stephen. He is currently taking an NVQ level 2 in direct care and plans to go on to develop his care and managerial skills. He hopes to work in day centres and progress to social work training later in his career.

Social work

A social worker is a person who has gained a professional social work qualification, (normally a Diploma in Social Work), and who has experience of working with clients with social, financial and emotional problems. The Diploma in Social Work is a two-year course of study and practical placements. Courses are run in further and higher education institutions and require a minimum of A level or GNVQ Advanced level qualifications, and some social care experience. Mature students over the age of 21 may gain a place on the basis of experience and other qualifications. Because of the difficult and stressful nature of the work, and the need for some maturity and life experience, most social work courses have a minimum entry age of 21.

Most professionally qualified social workers are employed as field social workers. This means that they have a caseload of people they work with in community and institutional settings.

CASE STUDY

The psychiatric social worker

Kimberley Taylor is a psychiatric social worker in a hospital accident and emergency department. She starts work at 9 a.m. every weekday morning. Her day can be unpredictable as she is never sure who will come in, or how they might need her help. People arrive with a variety of psychological problems. Kimberley receives referrals from the duty doctor and nurses in the department. She interviews all the people referred to her to assess their mental health needs and social problems. Following each assessment, she organises social care and support, in hospital or at home, and liaises with other care workers to ensure that care can be provided. During the week, Kimberley attends several meetings with colleagues to discuss the patients she has seen and the running of the department.

Some social workers specialise in working with particular types of clients, such as in child protection work or psychiatric social work, whereas others operate as generic social workers and see people referred to them with various problems.

Within social work, there is a grading structure through which people can progress as they gain experience and demonstrate their ability. Career opportunities can arise for social workers to become team leaders or to go into management and become care managers and, ultimately, directors of social services.

Social care

There is a range of vocationally qualified and non-qualified people who also work in social care settings in a support capacity. Like the health care support worker, social care

CASE STUDY

The child and family specialist

Michael Chan is a social worker employed by social services to work with children and families. He works a 9–5 day, with some evenings on call each month. He tries to provide a link between social care services and families in need of help and support. Each morning, Michael sees new referrals to assess their social needs. He tries to sort out any immediate financial or personal problems they have, and puts them in touch with other services, such as the Department of Social Security, which can give financial help. Each week he organises and runs case conferences for those clients who are to be discharged. At these meetings, all the care workers involved with a particular client meet with the client and his or her informal carers to discuss what care needs to be provided. As a placement tutor, Michael often has a student social worker with him and gives teaching sessions and support where necessary.

support workers now tend to have NVQ training gained through experience and work under the supervision of qualified social workers, often providing much practical help and support for clients and having much client contact.

Social care jobs are advertised by local authorities and voluntary and private-sector organisations in local and national papers. For some posts, previous experience and specific qualifications are required. Other posts require a relevant vocational qualification, such as GNVQ Intermediate Health and Social Care, and an aptitude for care work is requested. There is no official minimum age for entry into this type of care work. Like health care support worker posts, employers look for people with personal maturity and some life experience that gives them the ability to help and support others.

Social care jobs fall into three main areas:

- domiciliary, or home, care
- residential care
- day care.

Social care workers may work a variety of different shift patterns. Day care workers tend to work 9–5, Monday to Friday, domiciliary care workers may work at any time of the day from early morning to late evening, while residential social care workers may work day and night shifts and weekends.

CASE STUDY

The home carer and the residential social worker

Bhupinder Mann is employed as a home carer by a local authority. She works a shift system that includes days, nights and weekend work. She has undertaken NVQ level 2 training and has been on food hygiene and lifting and handling courses. She visits up to six different elderly clients in their homes each day. She helps them to wash and dress and prepares breakfast or an evening drink for them. Bhupinder enjoys the practical side of her job and feels that it is important to be well organised and understanding to do her job well.

Daniel McClaren is a residential social worker in a private children's home. He works shifts on a rota system, which means that he works two weekends per month, three months of nights each year, and day shifts in between. After gaining his GNVQ Intermediate Health and Social Care, he began an NVQ level 2 in Childcare with his local TEC. His placement experience at the children's home led to a full-time post. He is part of a care team that looks after six children when they are not at school. Daniel has special responsibility for organising the recreational and sports activities for the weekends and school holidays.

Childcare and early years education

Childcare and early years education are areas in which there is a wide range of care roles and career opportunities. Childcare and early years workers may have one or more qualifications or may gain work because of their own experience of bringing up children. NVQs in Childcare and Education are specifically designed to develop and assess skills gained by childcare workers in the workplace. Many nursery, playgroup and classroom assistants now undertake NVQ training.

Nursery nursing

A qualified nursery nurse has achieved a qualification such as an NNEB or BTEC Diploma in Nursery Nursing. Nursery nurses are employed in private and local authority nurseries, usually providing direct care and education for children under five.

Playgroup assistant

People who work as assistants in playgroups and nurseries work under the supervision of a nursery nurse or another experienced playgroup worker. Many carers take NVQ qualifications to improve their knowledge and skills. There are no minimum age requirements or specific qualifications required to gain entry to playgroup work.

Play specialist

Play specialists work with children in hospital. Their role is to use play as a means of developing children's practical and communication skills at a time in their lives when ordinary school life and opportunities to play with other children are limited by their illnesses or disabilities. Play specialists can take specialist courses to improve their knowledge and skills.

Early years teacher

Nursery and infant teachers work in state and private primary schools and have to achieve a degree qualification to obtain a post. They work with groups of children, planning and assessing learning activities for them, often using play to do this. Early years teachers work school hours and often work at home to prepare and mark work and do their record keeping.

Classroom assistant

Classroom assistants are not qualified teachers. They assist the teacher with practical activities, such as setting up the classroom and supervising children on outings, and help children with basic care tasks, such as changing their clothes and going to the toilet where they are unable to do so for themselves. Classroom assistants can take specialist courses and NVQs to improve their skills. They work school hours.

Registered childminder

Childminders work in their own home looking after one or more children, usually in office or other working hours when the children's parents are working. Childminders must be registered with their local authority and must be able to offer the facilities and experience needed to provide a good standard of care. The minimum age requirement for registered childminders is set down by the local authority and is usually 21.

Professions allied to medicine

Besides medicine and nursing, there are a number of other care roles within the health care occupational area. Examples include occupational therapy, physiotherapy, speech therapy and radiography. These are referred to as professions allied to medicine (PAMs). Practitioners in these areas generally work in multidisciplinary teams with medical, nursing and social work staff in both hospital and community settings.

People who train and work in the professions allied to medicine generally have a degree level qualification. Entrants to training courses require A level /GNVQ Advanced level qualifications and some care experience. Mature students over the age of 21 may be able to gain a place on the basis of their prior care experience and educational ability. There are also some opportunities to work as assistants to professionally qualified practitioners. These vacancies are advertised in professional magazines and local newspapers by NHS trusts and social services departments.

CASE STUDY

The radiographer

Jenny Field is a junior diagnostic radiographer at St Joseph's hospital. Her job involves taking X-rays of patients with fractures and internal problems and ultrasound scans of pregnant women. Jenny works shifts, including nights and weekends, at the hospital. To qualify, Jenny took a three-year diploma course in radiography at the hospital.

CASE STUDY

The physiotherapist and the occupational therapist

Darren Samuels is a self-employed physiotherapist. After gaining his degree in physiotherapy, he acquired experience as a basic grade and then senior physiotherapist in a district general hospital. Darren's role was to plan and carry out exercise, movement and massage programmes for patients who required rehabilitation following injuries and illnesses that affected their physical abilities. As a hospital-based physiotherapist, Darren worked weekdays, 9–5, seeing patients by referral from other professionals. Darren became self-employed, running his own practice, two years ago. He now sees patients by referral from other professionals and people who refer themselves. He works longer hours, including some evenings and Saturdays to fit in with his clients' lifestyles.

Rikki Starr works as a senior occupational therapist at the Highgrove Mental Health Centre. She assesses patients' social, psychological and physical needs and abilities. She then offers them programmes of activity and therapy designed to enable them to develop or regain practical skills and personal attributes, such as self-esteem and confidence, that increase their independence. Rikki undertook a degree course to gain her basic qualification and has since taken several short courses to improve her skills in management, counselling and artwork.

Administration, management and ancillary jobs

Health and social care organisations employ a wide range of support staff who carry out the administration, management and ancillary jobs that are essential for all organisations and direct care workers to work efficiently. Entry qualifications vary depending on the type of job. There are no specific minimum age requirements for administrative, management or ancillary jobs.

Administrative work covers secretarial and clerical jobs such as typing, filing, record keeping and wages calculations. Information technology, accountancy, typing and customer care courses are all available as NVQ courses through colleges and many training departments within care organisations.

Management work involves taking responsibility for the effective and efficient running of various aspects of a care organisation. People who work as managers may have specialist qualifications in the area in which they are working, such as medical laboratory science, an additional management qualification and experience gained through working in various posts. Managers have more power and responsibility than administrative staff and are usually responsible for a group of staff and a department. Managers usually work office hours, Monday to Friday. They have a variety of qualifications including NVQs, degrees and diplomas in different areas of management.

Ancillary work covers areas needed to keep a care organisation running effectively, such as catering, cleaning and maintenance. People who work as ancillary workers may have vocational qualifications appropriate to the area in which they work, such as catering or electrical work, or may obtain their jobs because of prior experience and the practical skills that they have. Ancillary workers work a variety of shift patterns with some working office hours while others work at night and at weekends to keep the care services operating.

CASE STUDY

The facilities manager, the accounting technician and the cleaner

Angela Bee is the facilities manager at St Joseph's hospital. She is responsible for the safe and efficient running of the catering, laundry, portering, maintenance and gardening services that operate behind the scenes at St Joseph's. Angela works with the staff in each of the areas mentioned, holds daily meetings to discuss staffing and operational issues, and liaises with other managers responsible for the direct care and financial aspects of running the hospital. Her job is mainly a 9–5 one, but she can be contacted to sort out problems that occur outside of office hours.

Eric Allman is an accounting technician working in the local authority finance department. He is responsible for monitoring and producing financial records of spending by the social services department through the contracts that it makes with various social care organisations. He works office hours, mainly in the finance office. He has undertaken an NVQ level 2 in Accountancy and is currently studying for an NVQ level 3 in Information Technology. He works office hours, Monday to Friday and is part of a team of workers in the finance section.

Anthea Johnson works as a domestic cleaner in the dermatology outpatient clinic attached to the hospital's burns unit. She works five days a week, 5 a.m. to 8 a.m. She is responsible for cleaning the floors, desks and other surfaces, and generally tidies the department each morning before other people arrive. Anthea is currently taking an NVQ level 2 in Cleaning.

Making career choices

Many people wish to work in health and social care jobs. When making decisions about which specialist area to enter, individuals need advice based on good research and up-to-date information. Sources of information include the national bodies of the different caring professions.

Within each occupational area of care work it is possible to progress in a number of different ways. Gaining basic qualifications and experience is the important first step in a career in care work. Finding out about the different ways in which your career might develop later as you gain experience is important when thinking about which area of care to enter. People like to progress in their careers. Having a good idea of the different possibilities at the beginning makes career planning easier and gives people an incentive to develop their skills in particular areas. Most care workers progress by gaining further qualifications and experience in specialist areas of their field.

Build your learning

Summary points

- The only way to qualify as a medical doctor is to obtain a university medical degree.

- A person must be seventeen and a half years of age and have obtained a minimum of five GCSEs (or equivalent) before he or she can begin registered nurse training.

- No specific qualifications are required to obtain a job as a health or social care support worker.

- Support workers can, and often do, obtain National Vocational Qualifications (NVQs) in care through their direct care work with patients and clients.

- Social workers are employed in a variety of settings and have usually obtained a Diploma in Social Work through a college-based training course.

- There is a wide range of jobs and qualifications in the childcare and early years sector. These range from NVQ to degree-level qualifications.

- People who work in the one of the professions allied to medicine have usually obtained a degree-level qualification.

Key words and phrases

You should know the meaning of the words and phrases listed below that relate to career routes and entry qualifications needed for health, social care and early years work. If you are not sure about any of them, go back through the last 15 pages to check and refresh your understanding.

- Junior house officer
- Registered nurse
- Staff nurse
- Project 2000
- Field social worker

- Health care support worker
- Diploma in Social Work
- Domiciliary care
- Nursery nurse

- Professions allied to medicine (PAMs)
- Radiographer
- Ancillary work
- Play specialist

Student questions

1 What qualifications are usually needed to obtain a place on a nurse training programme?

2 What are the professions allied to medicine (PAMs)? Name at least three of the main PAMs.

3 Where do domiciliary care workers carry out care work?

4 In your own words explain the difference between the jobs of registered nurse and health care support worker.

5 Name the qualification that is usually needed to get a job as a field social worker.

ASSESSMENT WORK

The roles of local care workers

Care organisations are staffed by people who perform a wide range of direct and indirect care roles. This activity gives you an opportunity to find out about the roles of two care workers in local care organisations. It is linked to the assessment work on page 34. The work that you do here will become a part of your end of unit assignment.

	Assessment criteria	Which tasks do I need to do?
Pass	Clearly describe the roles of two workers, explaining the care value base that would underpin their work.	2a 2b
Merit	Analyse the job roles to compare ways in which the care value base is implemented in different settings.	2c
Distinction	Show a high level of understanding of the care settings and the work roles of staff in the settings.	2a 2b 2c

If you carry out the following activities now, you will have completed some of the work needed for your end of unit assignment.

Key skills

C2.1b, C2.2, C2.3, IT2.2, IT2.3

It may be possible to claim these key skills for this coursework depending on how you have completed the tasks and presented your work. Your teacher will need to check your evidence against the key skills specification.

What to do

2a Identify and briefly describe the type of work role that two local care workers perform.

2b Describe how each of the care workers implement two aspects of the care value base in their day to day work (see page 68 for further information on the care value base).

2c Analyse each care worker's job role. Identify and compare the ways in which each role enables the care worker to implement the care value base.

To gain a distinction you will need to show 'a high level of understanding of the work roles of staff in the two care settings'.

Effective communication skills

Effective communication skills are a valuable asset in care and early years work. These skills help people working in health, social care and early years settings to pass on information clearly and concisely and to take part confidently in professional discussions with colleagues and clients. Care and early years workers need to develop skills that promote communication:

- between carers and clients
- between carers and clients' families
- among carers
- between managers and carers
- between caring services.

The communication process

Communication is something that occurs *between* people and is a two-way process. When people communicate, they pass on a message to another person or group of people in a language that the person or group understands. Figure 1.11 shows the communication cycle. There are three basic parts to this cycle.

- A person sends a message by using verbal and/or non-verbal methods.
- A second person, or group of people, receives the message through sight, touch and/or hearing.
- The receiver of the message usually responds, or gives feedback, to the sender.

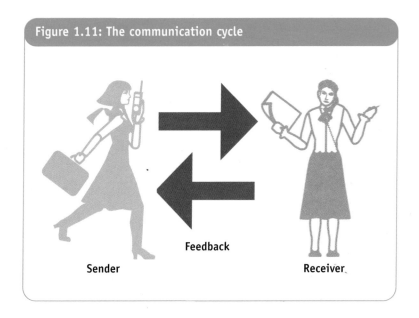

Figure 1.11: The communication cycle

Feedback

Sender

Receiver

Where a message is deliberately passed and consciously received with some response by the second person, there is said to be an **interpersonal interaction**.

Why communication skills are important in care work

If you were unable to communicate with other people, life would be very difficult. You would face considerable problems in meeting your basic physical, psychological and social needs. Similarly, if you are a care worker and communicate in a way that your colleagues, patients or clients fail to understand, you will not be able to identify and meet their needs or perform your job properly.

To be an effective communicator in a care setting you must remember that the purpose of the interaction, the client's stage of development and his or her level of understanding will affect how you communicate with the client. You need to make sure that the pace, level and manner of discussion are appropriate, to enable you to communicate effectively.

Figure 1.12: The benefits of effective communication

For the carers	For the patient or client
1 Good communication enables you to obtain and provide information that is relevant to your clients' care and well-being.	1 Good communication enables clients to feel secure and respected at times when they are physically and emotionally vulnerable.
2 Good communication enables you to express the important values of acceptance, trust, understanding and support.	2 Cooperation, involvement and partnership in a caring relationship require open, supportive communication.
3 Through good communication you can enable your clients to make the most of their abilities and personal resources.	3 Effective communication allows the client to express his or her needs, worries and wishes.
4 Good communication allows you to choose the most effective means of meeting your clients' needs.	4 Clients need to maintain their sense of personal identity. This can only be achieved if they are allowed to express themselves and be understood by their carers.

The benefits of effective communication

Good communication in care settings helps both carers and clients in the care relationship that develops between them. Figure 1.12 describes some of the benefits of effective communication from each point of view. You may wish to add others that occur to you or which your experience, as either a carer or client, has highlighted as important.

Methods of communication

People use a number of methods to communicate in health and social care settings. The methods of sending messages can be divided into verbal and non-verbal forms. Verbal communication includes pitch and tone of voice, language, and pauses and silences, non-verbal communication includes body language, clothing and appearance. Receiving messages involves listening and observation skills.

How verbal communication is used in care settings

Effective verbal communication involves speaking and listening to others. Care workers need to be able to communicate effectively with their colleagues and managers, with patients and clients and their families. Effective communication skills are needed to participate in conversations, interviews, and meetings where care workers give and receive information, provide support and build up their relationships with clients and colleagues. To be effective in care settings, verbal communication messages should be conveyed clearly in ways that are supportive to clients and that respect their rights and personal values.

How non-verbal communication is used in care settings

Non-verbal communication is very important in enabling care workers to build and maintain their relationships with patients and clients. Most first impressions are gained from non-verbal communication. The clothes, appearance, posture, tone of voice and amount of eye contact that we use all say something about us to people when we meet for the first time.

Clients and patients, like everybody else, are continually monitoring their interactions with care staff for the non-verbal communication of feelings, preferences and confirmation of verbal messages. Carers need to use their non-verbal behaviours carefully to establish and maintain positive relationships with their patients or clients. Non-verbal signals are often a more powerful means of communicating messages than verbal signals.

When non-verbal messages are at odds with the things that people say, the listener is more likely to believe the non-verbal message that he or she receives. If care workers form a negative impression of a patient or client, for example as a 'difficult' or unlikeable person, this may be expressed in their non-verbal behaviour rather than through what they say to the individual. Disapproving facial expressions or avoiding being close to the person would tell the patient or client that he or she is not liked by the care worker.

▼ Non-verbal messages can be as clear as verbal communication

ACTIVITY

Effective communication

Care workers need to use a variety of communication methods with patients and clients. The primary aim of all caring is to meet the needs of those being cared for.

Read the scenarios on the next page. For each one, explain briefly which communication methods could be used to best help the person.

- Salvo is a patient in the medical ward of a large district general hospital. His diabetes has progressively worsened and he has now lost his sight. He finds this very distressing and tends to stay close to his bed for fear of getting lost in the ward. He asks you if you will take him to the toilet. He stretches out his hand and gently moves to the edge of his bed. He tells you that he's sorry to ask but he's worried about getting there in time on his own.

- Edith is 56 years old and has recently suffered a stroke. This has left her with paralysis down her right-hand side and limited speech. She cannot put her thoughts into words or understand words that are written down but she can understand some of what is said to her. You have been asked to find out what she would like to choose from next week's menu. You have been given a printed menu which patients would normally fill in themselves.

- Philip has been in a psychiatric hospital for the last ten years. He has recently moved to the group home where you work as a residential worker. Today it is Philip's turn to go to the supermarket to get the weekend shopping for the five residents. He has limited experience of shopping and managing money and asks you, 'What do I have to do?'

- Kamlesh has hardly seen anybody other than her husband and children since the birth of her twin daughters six months ago. Her husband says that she rarely goes out and is becoming depressed because of her lack of contact with other women. You are a volunteer at a local playgroup and have been asked to visit Kamlesh to try and befriend her and persuade her to come along.

- Suman is seven years old. He goes to a behavioural support unit during the day. His behaviour at home is reckless, aggressive and very unsettled. He was sent to the unit after he climbed on to the roof of his local shopping arcade and began throwing down tiles at passers-by. He does not understand why he has to attend the unit. You have been asked to explain this to him without being critical of him personally.

5084.

Barriers to communication

When we communicate, our ability to get our message across effectively to others can be hampered by a number of barriers. As a care worker you will need to recognise barriers to your own communication and learn how to overcome them. In health, social care and early years settings these barriers include:

- language
- culture
- age
- disability
- illness.

Language

As a multiethnic society, the United Kingdom has many citizens whose first language is not English and who may find English difficult to understand. Many native speakers of English also find the complicated medical words on hospital signs and the jargon of health care workers hard to understand. In all of these circumstances, language can be an obstacle to effective communication between care workers and their patients and clients.

Culture

When we communicate with others we often take it for granted that the other person's culture (see page 204) is similar to, or the same as, our own. In a multiethnic society like the United Kingdom there are a lot of cultural differences between different groups in the population. These differences can affect the way people communicate and interact and can, at times, cause communication problems. For example, the amount of eye contact, the physical closeness or proximity and the amount of touching that people do when they communicate varies according to culture. It is important to be aware of this when working with people in care settings in order to make your communication with them effective.

Age

Age differences between care workers and their patients and clients can act as a barrier to communication where there is a generation gap that makes it hard for people to relate to each other. For example, young care staff may, without thinking, adopt a very informal, familiar approach when addressing and talking to the older people for whom they care. It is not unusual for some older residents in nursing homes to object when young, new and unfamiliar staff use their first names or

▼ Bilingual health care information

talk to them in a very informal way. In other situations patients and clients prefer informality. Children and teenagers would probably feel intimidated by care staff who talk to them in a formal, unfamiliar way. It is always necessary to find out from patients and clients how they prefer to be addressed and to adapt your communication skills to their needs.

Disability and illness

The disabilities, impairments and illnesses that some patients and clients experience can make communication more difficult unless care workers find ways of adapting to them. For example, people who have sensory impairments (visual, hearing or both) may have difficulty with the spoken or non-verbal aspects of communication, depending on their particular impairment. People who have learning disabilities may struggle to understand the content of communications that include complex, difficult language and words or ideas that they are not familiar with. Care workers should always try to empathise with the person with whom they are aiming to communicate. They should try and work out how to get their message across to the person in the most effective way.

Build your learning

Summary points

- All care workers need to be able to communicate effectively with patients and clients.

- Communication involves the sending and receiving of verbal and non-verbal messages.

- Both care workers and their patients and clients benefit from effective communication.

- A variety of factors, including language difficulties, cultural differences and problems caused by illness and impairment, can present barriers to effective communication.

Key words and phrases

You should know the meaning of the words and phrases listed below that relate to basic ideas about, and methods of, communication. If you are not sure about any of them, go back through the last seven pages to check and refresh your understanding.

- Communication
- Interpersonal interaction
- Communication cycle

- Interpersonal skills
- Verbal communication
- Non-verbal communication

- Eye contact
- Gesture
- Communication barrier

 Student questions

1 In your own words, explain what happens during the communication cycle.

2 Why do care workers need to be effective communicators? Give at least three reasons.

3 What is non-verbal communication?

4 Give an example of the way in which communication can occur through non-verbal methods in a care setting.

5 'Care workers should always be aware of possible barriers to communication when dealing with patients or clients.' What kind of things can act as barriers, or obstacles, to effective communication in care settings?

ASSESSMENT WORK

Communicating in care settings

Communication is a very important part of any care worker's role. This activity gives you an opportunity to demonstrate that you understand the importance of communication skills and that you can communicate effectively in care settings. The work that you do here can be used as part of your end of unit assignment. The table below indicates which tasks you have to complete to have a chance of gaining a pass, merit or distinction grade.

	Assessment criteria	Which tasks do I need to do?
Pass	Demonstrate relevant communication skills and describe possible barriers to communication.	3a
Merit	Evaluate your communication strategies, identifying strengths and ways to improve on weaknesses.	3a 3b
Distinction	Use language with fluency, showing communication skills appropriate to vocational settings.	3a 3b 3c

What to do

 Use role plays or your work placement to demonstrate your understanding of, and skills in, communication in care settings.

- **Demonstrate that you can communicate effectively with a client on a one-to-one basis. You could choose one of the situations on pages 62–3 to role play with a partner.**

- **Demonstrate that you are able to use your communication skills in a group situation with clients or colleagues. You could allocate roles and role-play a meeting at the health centre (see page 12), for example.**

 In each of the situations, identify the strengths of the communication skills that you used.

 What areas do you feel that you need to improve on? Suggest how might you be able to do this.

Key skills

C2.1a, C2.3

It may be possible to claim these key skills for this coursework depending on how you have completed the tasks and presented your work. Your teacher will need to check your evidence against the key skills specification.

The care value base

Care workers should understand and always try to express appropriate values in their work with patients and clients. A **value** is a belief about what is morally right. For example, a care assistant working with older people might say, 'I try to improve the quality of older people's lives'. A social worker working with children and families might say, 'I try to treat all people equally, whoever they are'. A counsellor might say 'It's important to keep the things my clients talk to me about confidential'. We all have beliefs about what is important and right in care work.

The values of good care practice

Make a list of all those values that you feel should be part of good care practice. Try to come up with lists of examples to illustrate the values that you identify.

Care values in practice

The care value base identifies a series of values that care workers should try to express in their work with patients, clients and their families and colleagues. These include:

- maintaining the confidentiality of information
- promoting and supporting individuals' rights to dignity, independence, choice of health and safety
- acknowledging individuals' personal beliefs and identity
- supporting individuals through alternative approaches
- promoting anti-discriminatory practice.

Maintaining the confidentiality of information

People's relationships are based on the trust that they have in each other. If you cannot trust another person with your thoughts and feelings then your relationship with him or her is likely to be quite superficial. The caring relationship is also based on trust and the need for care workers to maintain **confidentiality** whenever possible. Confidentiality is an important but very difficult issue in care work. Decisions to disclose information that breaches confidentiality should never be taken lightly and each situation must be thought through individually. Your decision on whether to keep or breach confidentiality can be arrived at by following the guidelines below.

▼ Confidentiality is a vital element in the caring relationship

Keeping things to yourself

There are times when it is important to keep confidences and information that you have about clients to yourself. For example, if a child at the nursery where you do your work placement swore at you and misbehaved one afternoon, or an elderly resident at a nursing home refused to bathe after wetting herself, you would be breaching confidentiality to reveal these things to your friends. You should not breach confidentiality in situations where:

- people have a right to privacy
- their comments or behaviour do not cause anybody harm or break the law.

Where care workers gossip or talk publicly about their clients they are betraying the trust that has been put in them.

Telling other people

There are other times when you must reveal what you have been told, or have seen, to a more senior person at work.

69

Where clients request that you keep what they tell you a secret, this can be overridden if:

- what they reveal involves them breaking the law or planning to do so
- they tell you that they intend to harm themselves or another person
- they reveal information that can be used to protect another person from harm.

If an offence is committed that could have been prevented by your revealing the confidence, you could be brought to court to face charges. Care workers should never promise a client that what they say will be absolutely confidential. They should explain that, depending on what they are told or observe, there are times when they may have to share information with their colleagues and other authorities.

ACTIVITY

Confidentiality or disclosure

Read the following situations.

- Darren has an appointment with the college nurse for a BCG booster. He's worried about it making him ill. He says that he's just taken some ecstasy and pleads with the nurse not to tell anyone.

- Jennifer goes to her GP for contraceptive pills. She asks her GP not to tell her parents. She is 14 years old.

- Eileen has terminal cancer. She tells her district nurse that she's had enough of living and is going to end her own life tomorrow. She says it's her choice and asks the district nurse not to interfere.

- Yasmin tells her new health visitor that her boyfriend is violent and is beating her. She asks the health visitor not to say anything as she is frightened of what might happen. Yasmin and her boyfriend have a three-month-old baby.

- Lee turns up at a hostel for the homeless. He says that he has run away from home because his father is beating him. He asks the social worker not to contact his family. He is 16 years old.

- A social worker phones Terry's teacher to ask whether she knows anything about his home life. The social worker explains that she is worried about Terry's stepfather. Terry is six years old.

- A man with a stab wound arrives at the hospital casualty department. He won't give his name and asks the nurse not to phone the police. He says that he will leave if she does. He is bleeding heavily.

- Ian is visited in hospital by his local priest. He is recovering from an overdose of tablets. He confesses to the priest that he knocked over a girl on the zebra crossing in town. The girl is still in a coma. Ian says he can't live with himself. The police have appealed for information on the car driver.

Draw a line down the middle of a blank piece of paper. The top end of the line is 'absolute confidentiality', the bottom end is 'complete disclosure'. Write each of the client's names on the part of the line that indicates the degree of confidentiality you feel is appropriate to each case. Write a short paragraph on each client explaining:

- why confidentiality may be important to the client

- the dilemma facing the care worker

- the reasons for your decision about confidentiality.

Discuss your answers with other members of your class. Make brief notes on points of view that are different to your own.

Promoting and supporting individuals' rights

The relationship that you develop with the patients or clients with whom you will work is the cornerstone of all the work that you will do as a care provider. It is good practice on the part of carers and care organisations to enable clients to have **choices** about their care and to make their own decisions. Ideally, care workers and clients should develop a partnership relationship in which the client feels equally involved. These kinds of care relationship are **empowering** because they regard people as:

- valid and important in their own right
- having rights and choices appropriate to their age and needs
- deserving of respect, regardless of their personal or social characteristics.

Positive, empowering relationships depend on care workers using communication skills effectively in their interactions with clients. Being sensitive to what other people are saying, thinking and feeling, treating them with respect, and protecting their dignity and rights, are all features of empowering care practice. To be able to do these things, care workers need to be sensitive to the spoken and unspoken communication of their clients. They also need to be aware of how they themselves think, feel and behave in their interactions with clients.

Looking after people is only one part of care work. On its own, this approach may result in the client becoming dependent on the carer. Good care practice also involves the carer working to promote the rights, independence and development of the client.

ACTIVITY

Experiences of care situations

We all have expectations of how we should be treated by care workers when we use care services. You have probably had good and bad experiences in your contacts with care workers. This activity requires you to identify why one relationship with a care worker was positive and why another was negative.

Think of two contacts you have had with health or social care workers. One should be a positive experience and the other a negative experience. You might refer to your contact with a doctor, a hospital worker, a dentist, a counsellor or social worker who you've seen. You don't have to use their real names or disclose any details about your reasons for seeing them.

Think of all the reasons why one experience was positive and one was negative, giving examples under the following headings.

- How did they empower/disempower you?
- How did they acknowledge/fail to acknowledge your personal beliefs?
- How did they build up/reduce your self-esteem?

Discuss your positive and negative experiences in a small group. As a group, discuss the ideas that you all have and bring them together as a list of ten ways to promote a positive relationship with clients. Write your ideas down on a large sheet of paper and explain them to the rest of the class.

Acknowledging people's personal beliefs and identity

Acknowledging people's personal beliefs and identity means that care workers should try to communicate that they accept people for who they are and what they believe in. Care workers may not always share the beliefs and lifestyle of the people they care for but should still show that they accept their clients' individuality. For example, if you care for people who have different religious beliefs and practices to your own, you should give them the opportunity to practise their faith and celebrate their religious festivals at times when this is important to them.

Supporting people through alternative approaches

Care workers need to be flexible and resourceful in trying to find ways of helping and supporting their patients and clients. They should continually look for new ways of caring for them. This can be especially important where a person does not benefit from an established or standard approach. It involves seeing the individual's needs and well-being as the focus of care work rather than being committed to a long-established timetable or traditional way of doing things in a care setting. Care workers should always work to promote their patients' and clients' interests in the most effective ways possible.

Promoting anti-discriminatory practice

Care workers who adopt an anti-discriminatory approach to their care work need to be:

- aware of the different forms of unfair discrimination that can occur
- sensitive to the ethnic and social background and cultural needs of each individual for whom they provide care
- prepared to actively challenge and work towards reducing the unfair discrimination experienced by their patients or clients.

People experience unfair discrimination because of their race or colour (racism), gender (sexism), age (ageism), disability, sexuality (homophobia), religion or health status. Carers should never unfairly discriminate against the people whom they care for. It is always best to follow codes of practice and charters (see page 76) that set out principles of good practice to ensure that this is avoided. Wherever they receive care, all patients and clients are entitled to non-discriminatory treatment. Anti-discriminatory practice does not mean treating everybody the same. It means recognising and responding to the individual needs of patients and clients.

The experience of unfair discrimination

Unfair discrimination occurs when individuals or groups of people are treated differently, unequally and unfairly in comparison to others. Unfair discrimination involves a person acting on his or her prejudices. For example, an employer who refused to interview candidates under the age of 25 for a nursery manager post saying 'in my experience, younger people are not good at accepting responsibility', would be treating this group of people unfairly.

There are times when it is fair to discriminate between people. For example, when deciding which applicant for a job should be appointed an interviewer is justified in discriminating fairly between the candidates by choosing the best person for the job. He or she can decide fairly by comparing each candidate's qualifications, experience and ability to do the work involved.

The main cause of unfair discrimination is prejudice. Prejudice involves experiencing negative or hostile feelings and having negative ideas and hostile attitudes towards other people. Prejudiced feelings, ideas and attitudes have no basis in fact and are not thought through by the person holding them.

When people are prejudiced they are often prejudiced against specific groups of people. In the United Kingdom, some of the groups which tend to experience unfair discrimination include:

- minority ethnic groups
- minority religious groups
- women
- lesbians and gay men
- older people
- the learning and physically disabled
- people with mental health problems.

Promoting equality of opportunity in care settings

Equality means being equal. **Equality of opportunity** means having the same chance of gaining access to, or use of, something. Over the last decade, care workers and politicians have increasingly stressed the importance of promoting equality of opportunity, protecting and maintaining clients' rights and ensuring that people are able to make choices and decisions about their own care.

To help make sure that carers respect clients' rights, codes of practice and policies have been developed and are used in many care settings.

Codes of practice and charters

A **code of practice** is a document that outlines an agreed way of working and dealing with specified situations. Codes of practice aim to reflect and set a standard for good practice in care settings. A number of codes of practice have been developed for care workers such as registered nurses, occupational and physiotherapists, social workers and nursery staff. Codes of practice establish the general principles and standards for care workers and should always refer to equality of opportunity.

A **policy** is different to a code of practice in that it tells care workers how they should do specific things in particular care settings. A code of practice for registered nurses applies to all registered nurses working in care settings. A policy on dealing with a missing patient, for example, will tell a registered nurse working in the particular care setting where the policy applies how to deal with this situation. Policies should also promote equal treatment and equality of opportunity for everyone likely to be affected by them.

The Patients' Charter

The Patients' Charter is part of a government initiative that aims to raise standards in public sector services. It sets out the patients' rights and the standards of service that they can expect from statutory health and social care organisations. The Patients' Charter focuses on all aspects of service and sets minimum performance standards, such as how soon emergency ambulances should arrive when called and how long it should take to get an operation in an NHS hospital.

Figure 1.13: The Patients' Charter: example of standards

Every patient has the right to:

- choose whether or not they take part in medical research or student training

- access to their health records and the knowledge that everyone working for the NHS is under a legal duty to keep them confidential

- change their GP easily and quickly

- have any complaint about NHS services investigated and to receive a quick, full, written reply from the relevant chief executive

- be admitted to hospital within 18 months of referral.

Every patient can expect:

- to be given a specific appointment time to be seen at a hospital outpatient clinic and be seen within 30 minutes of that time

- all the staff they meet to wear name badges

- a mutually convenient appointment within a two-hour time band for any home visit by a community nurse, health visitor or midwife.

Nursing

Nursing and Midwifery Admissions Service,
Rosehill, New Barn Lane,
Cheltenham,
Gloucestershire GL52 3LZ

English National Board for Nursing and Midwifery,
Victory House,
170 Tottenham Court Road,
London W1P 0HA

National Board for Scotland,
22 Queen Street,
Edinburgh EH2 1NT

Northern Ireland National Board,
Centre House,
79 Chichester Street,
Belfast BT1 4JE

Welsh National Board,
Second Floor
Golate House,
101 St Mary Street,
Cardiff CF1 1DX

Professions allied to medicine

British College of Occupational Therapy,
106–114 Borough High Street,
London SE1 1LB

The Chartered Society of Physiotherapy,
14 Bedford Row,
London WC1R 4ED

Society and College of Radiographers,
2 Carriage Row,
183 Eversholt Street
London NW1 1BU

Promoting health and well-being 2

This unit will help you to develop your knowledge and understanding of some of the common factors that contribute to a person's health and well-being. You will learn about:

- definitions of health and well-being

- aspects of health and well-being that differ between different people and groups of people

- common factors that affect health and well-being and the different effects they can have

- physical measures that can be used to measure good health.

As a care student, and future care worker, health and well-being are terms that you should

understand. It is important that you are able to identify what good health involves and that you have an understanding of some of the measures of health that are used by care workers. You should be able to appreciate and explain the effects of a person's lifestyle on his or her health and well-being. Learning about different lifestyle practices that may put an individual's health at risk, and about the ways in which health promotion information can be provided to different sections of the population, will be of benefit if you chose to work with people in care situations.

The material covers Unit 2, Promoting Health and Well-being, of the GNVQ Intermediate full award and the GNVQ Intermediate Part One award.

Promoting health and well-being

In Unit 1 we looked at the different types of care services and organisations in the United Kingdom (see pages 4–38). Health care workers in hospitals and clinics spend most of their time dealing with disease and illness that has already happened. For example, people go to the hospital casualty unit or to their GP when they experience a disease, illness or injury. Health care staff then try to deal with their problems to make them 'healthy' again. In this unit we look at other ways of helping people to achieve health and well-being. In particular, we'll be looking at what health promotion involves and at how this can help people to prevent illness and disease from occurring in the first place.

Health promotion involves different ways of providing information to people to enable them to improve their health and well-being. In order to achieve this goal, the person planning the health promotion activity needs to have a clear definition of health and well-being.

Defining health and well-being

The first topic that we need to think about when we're exploring health promotion are the ideas of health and well-being themselves. These terms mean different things to different people. To one person, health may mean not having any injuries or diseases or simply not feeling unwell. This is known as a negative view of health because being healthy is based on not being unwell! An alternative, positive view of health involves identifying the qualities and abilities that a person ought to possess in order to be healthy. Being able to walk, run and carry out everyday tasks and responsibilities effortlessly might be seen as evidence that a person is healthy.

▶ Keeping fit

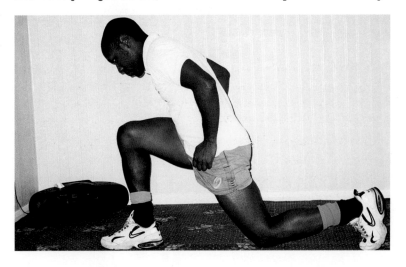

You should be aware that individuals' health needs vary according to the life stage they are in. For example, an active 16-year-old boy could be said to be just as healthy as his 70-year-old grandfather, who has much less physical energy. Individuals' health and well-being needs depend on factors such as their age, sex, gender, physical ability, occupation, religion, culture and other personal circumstances. We will look at how health needs differ throughout the life span on page 95.

The World Health Organisation takes a positive view when it defines health as 'a state of complete physical, mental and social well-being, not merely the absence of disease or infirmity' (WHO, 1946). When we take a positive view of health it is necessary to look at all aspects of an individual's life. This is usually referred to as an holistic approach. We must therefore consider all the following aspects of health.

Physical health:	refers to the efficient working of the body.
Social health:	is the individual's relationships with other people and related socioeconomic factors including education, employment, income and housing.
Intellectual health:	involves the individual's ability to learn, think and make judgements.
Emotional health:	refers to the individual's ability to recognise his or her own feelings and to express them appropriately.
Psychological health:	this term is used to cover the last two areas.
Mental health:	involves the ability to think clearly and coherently and to cope with everyday life and problems.

The idea of well-being

The term well-being is used to refer to the way people feel about themselves. If people feel good about themselves they will have a high level of well-being, and vice versa. Individuals are the best judges of their own sense of well-being. If they have good, supportive relationships and are confident that their basic material needs (for food, shelter and warmth) are going to be met, then they are likely to have a deeper and more lasting sense of well-being.

Illness, disease, ill health and sickness

The terms illness, disease and ill health are commonly used when people talk or write about health topics. Often these three terms are used in the same way to refer to an 'unhealthy' state. However, there are important distinctions between them. Disease is a term used by doctors and other health care workers to refer to an observable physical change in the body's correct structure or way of working. An illness is a subjective experience. This means that a person with an illness may complain that he or she feels unwell and has symptoms such as aches and pains, but these things can't be directly seen or observed by others.

People can have a disease (a change in their body) without feeling ill or noticing that anything is wrong. This is one of the reasons for having screening programmes. Cervical smears, breast screening after the age of 50, childhood blood tests and chest X-rays are all carried out to identify diseases that, in their early stages, often don't cause people to feel ill.

ACTIVITY

Healthy lifestyles?

The six people described in the case study on pages 87 and 88 have different lifestyles, attitudes, values and needs. In some ways they may be healthy, in other ways they may not. Read through each description and answer the questions that follow.

1 In what way is each person healthy or unhealthy? Make some notes of your own ideas. You might want to give each person a score (10 = extremely healthy, 1 = extremely unhealthy) for physical, emotional, social and intellectual health.

2 Discuss your ideas and scores with other people in the class.

3 What sort of approach to health are you using in making your decision about each person? (Hint: is your approach to health positive, negative or other?)

CASE STUDY

Denise, age 30, has a job as a stock broker. She buys and sells shares and must reach certain targets each week. She works out at the company gym each morning and then works very hard from 7.30 a.m. to 7.30 p.m. five days a week. She admits to feeling stressed most of the time. Before going home she usually goes for a few drinks with her colleagues to wind down. She has made a lot of money but says that she has little time for other things.

Robbie is a 27-year-old packer in a factory. He says that his job is very boring. His life really revolves around sport and fitness training. He goes to a gym five nights a week to do weight training. Before work each day he jogs or swims. He cycles everywhere he goes. Robbie is very concerned about his diet and his physical appearance. He thinks about exercise even when he isn't doing it. He always wants to do more to improve his body. He has recently started taking anabolic steroids to help him build up his physique.

Samira describes herself as 'just a housewife'. She is 23 and has two children under five. She lives on income support but occasionally gets help from her mother who lives a few miles away. She says that the children take up most of her time so she doesn't go out very often. Her favourite past time is television. After the children are in bed she likes to watch soap operas and quiz shows with a box of chocolates, some crisps and a few cans of lemonade.

Belinda is a 19-year-old student of geology. She joined the rock climbing group at her university and went on most of the climbing trips in her first year. She recently went on a trip to Snowdonia. This time, she says, she 'just lost her nerve'. She got stuck on a cliff face and had to be taken off by rescue helicopter. She has been feeling 'on edge' ever since. She has fallen behind in her studies this term.

Andy, age 47, gave up his job as a business studies lecturer two years ago to live in France and write books. He used to spend a lot of time out of doors, cycling around the countryside. Last year he damaged his ankle in a fall and can't ride far any more. Although he has made a few friends, he rarely has enough money to go out. Last winter he felt lonely. He caught pneumonia because he couldn't afford to heat his house. He is now working as a tourist guide to make some money until he gets a book published.

George is a 55-year-old nurse on a medical ward at the hospital. He works seven days a week, sometimes doing two seven-hour shifts (one in the morning the other in the afternoon) and finishing at 9.30 p.m. He is very concerned about hygiene. He always uses disposable gloves at work. He washes his hands several times during the day. He carries an extra suit of clothing to change into between shifts. He is worried that he might contract a serious disease and insists that his house is cleaned every day, with a fresh set of bed linen put on every other day. His spare time is spent sleeping.

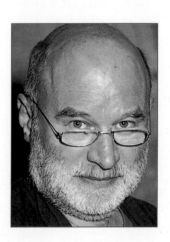

Health promotion agents

Everyone is responsible to some extent for their own health. However, health care practitioners and the government have a particular responsibility to give health information and to support people who are trying to live healthier lives.

Health promotion is a growing area of practice for health care workers. Most would probably say that the aim of their work is to help people to become healthy. Doctors, nurses and other care practitioners do give a lot of information and advice to the individuals with whom they come into contact. The health information and advice that health care workers give, and which the general public receive, tends to be part of government programmes to improve the nation's health.

One of the key things that the government does is to set health targets for health care practitioners to achieve. In June 1991, the government identified a number of national health targets. These were set out in a document called *The Health of the Nation*. This document set out an overall, national strategy for improving the health of the entire population by the year 2000.

The Health of the Nation

The Health of the Nation identified national targets in key health areas where the government felt that big improvements could be made. The key areas were:

- coronary heart disease and stroke
- cancers
- mental illness
- HIV/AIDS
- accidents.

Coronary heart disease, stroke and cancers were selected because there is scope for preventing illness and death from these conditions. Some, but not all, cancers can be prevented and others can be cured or controlled if individuals are screened and their cancers are detected early. Mental illness was selected because it affects a wide section of the population, both young and old, and the harm that it can cause can be reduced by improved services. HIV/AIDS was included as it is the greatest new threat to public health this century. Accidents are the most common cause of death in adults aged 16–30. Accidents are also an important cause of injury and disability among young children aged three to nine years and the elderly aged over 65 years. Many accidents are preventable.

The targets in the Health of the Nation plan include:

- reducing death rates for both coronary heart disease and stroke in people under 65 by at least 40 per cent by the year 2000
- reducing the death rate from breast cancer in women aged 50–64 by at least 25 per cent by the year 2000
- reducing cervical cancer by at least 20 per cent by the year 2005
- reducing the death rate for lung cancer by at least 30 per cent in men under 75 and 15 per cent in women under 75 by the year 2010
- reducing the overall suicide rate by at least 15 per cent
- reducing the suicide rate of severely mentally ill people by at least 33 per cent
- reducing the incidence of HIV infection, and sexually transmitted disease
- reducing the death rate for accidents among children under 15 by at least 33 per cent by 2005
- reducing the death rate for accidents among young people aged 15–24 by at least 25 per cent by 2005.

During the 1990s, some improvement in these areas has been achieved and maintained, but there is still much work to be done. Government health promotion activities and a variety of initiatives have been put into practice throughout the country. These have included cervical and breast screening programmes, health education campaigns (encouraging healthy eating and tackling alcohol-related problems, for example), targets for physical activity and campaigns to tackle teenage and adult smoking. In 1999, in its budget, the government maintained the high level of taxes on tobacco products and alcohol. This can also be seen as health promotion because it is a way of discouraging people from smoking and drinking excessive amounts of alcohol.

The main approach used in the health promotion campaigns linked to the Health of the Nation programme was to encourage people to live a healthier lifestyle. By taking personal responsibility for improving our diet (more fruit, less fat, less salt), getting more exercise, and drinking and smoking less, it was suggested that we could be healthier. The health promotion programmes were generally based on the idea that being healthier was the responsibility of, and could be influenced by, the individual.

The latest government approach to health promotion recognises that this isn't always the case.

Figure 2.1: Adults' views of what is bad for their health

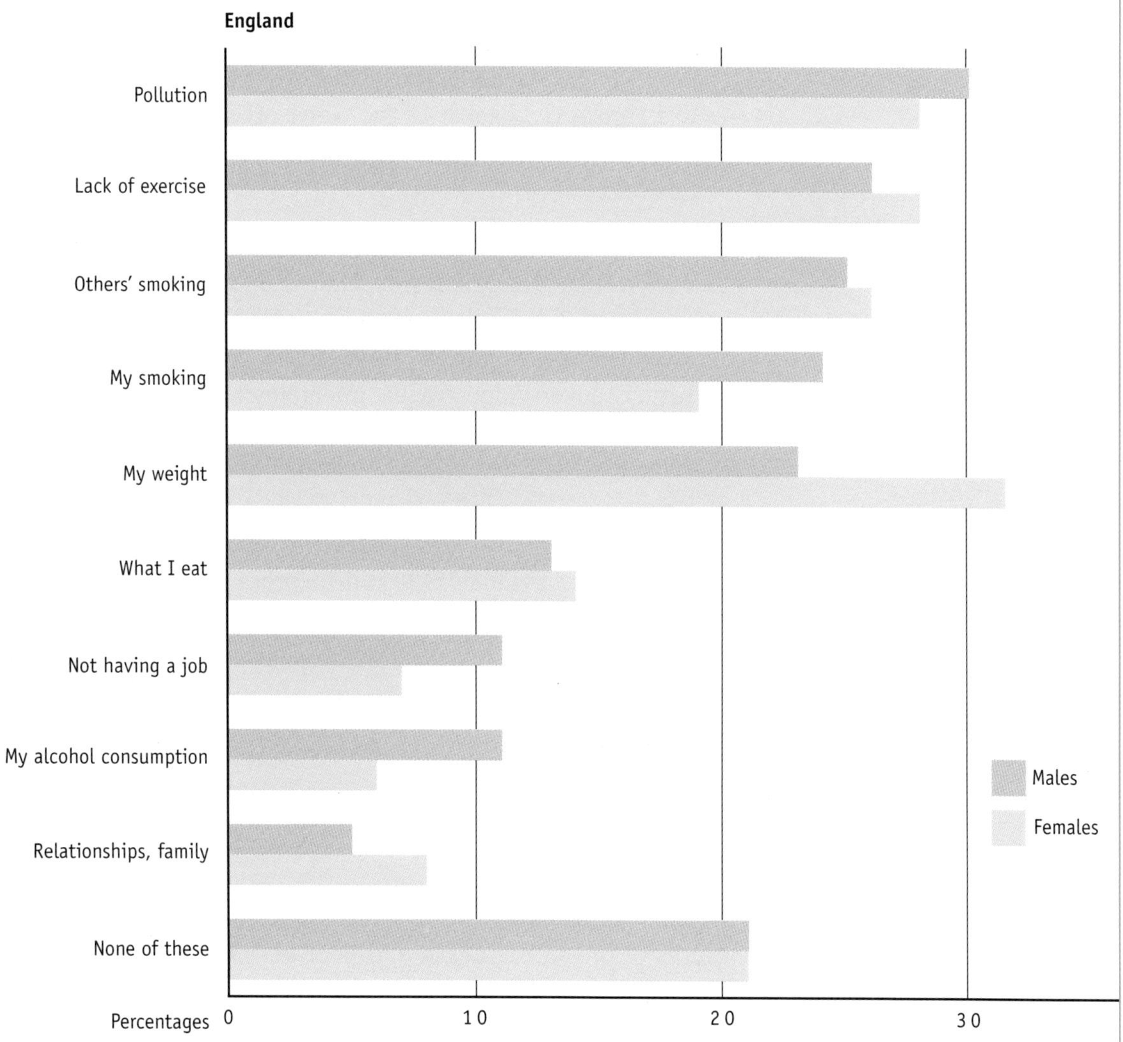
England
Pollution
Lack of exercise
Others' smoking
My smoking
My weight
What I eat
Not having a job
My alcohol consumption
Relationships, family
None of these
Percentages
0
10
20
30
Males
Females

Note: Adults surveyed in England, 1996

Source: Office for National Statistics and Health Education Authority

Our Healthier Nation

In February 1998, the Labour government published a new plan to promote health. It was called *Our Healthier Nation*. Health promotion departments and statutory health care services throughout the United Kingdom are now working toward achieving the aims of this new plan. In it, the government spells out its aims for improving the health and well-being of the worst off and the least healthy in society and for improving their neighbourhoods.

The main aims of the Our Healthier Nation programme are:

- to improve the health of the population as a whole by increasing the length of people's lives and the number of years people spend free from illness
- to improve the health of the worst off in society and to narrow the health gap that exists between different groups in society.

There are some things which affect health, such as housing and environmental conditions, that people have little personal control over. The government now wants to see far more attention concentrated on these factors. For example, air pollution, poverty, low wages, unemployment, poor housing, and crime and disorder are all factors that are largely beyond individual control but which can make people ill in both mind and body.

The government hopes that local agencies, communities, families and individuals will join together and work in partnership to improve the nation's health by tackling deep-seated health-related problems. Four main priority areas have been identified:

- heart disease and stroke
- accidents
- cancer
- mental health.

These areas have been selected because they are important causes of premature death and poor health. There are social inequalities, or differences, in who suffers from them. For example, poorer people and those living in deprived areas are more likely to suffer from cancer, heart disease and related illnesses, while people from wealthier, better off areas are more likely to survive cancer. The government feels that there is much that can be done to prevent these diseases and to improve effective treatment for all people who suffer them.

In order to address the key priority areas of Our Healthier Nation, health promotion activity is concentrated on three different settings:

- healthy schools – focusing on children
- healthy workplaces – focusing on adults
- healthy neighbourhoods – focusing on older people.

Figure 2.2: Major causes of mortality

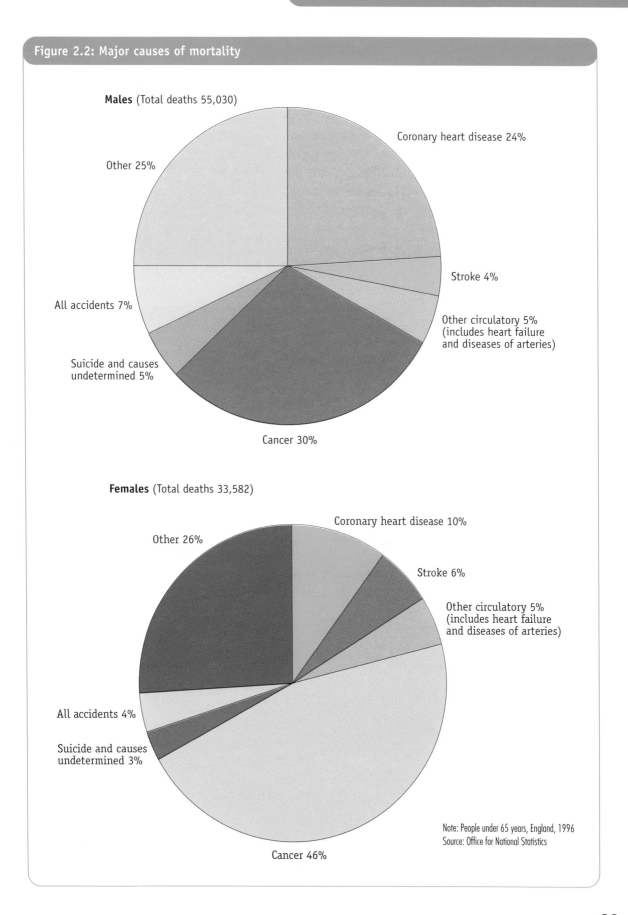

Males (Total deaths 55,030)

Coronary heart disease 24%

Other 25%

Stroke 4%

All accidents 7%

Other circulatory 5%
(includes heart failure
and diseases of arteries)

Suicide and causes
undetermined 5%

Cancer 30%

Females (Total deaths 33,582)

Coronary heart disease 10%

Other 26%

Stroke 6%

Other circulatory 5%
(includes heart failure
and diseases of arteries)

All accidents 4%

Suicide and causes
undetermined 3%

Cancer 46%

Note: People under 65 years, England, 1996
Source: Office for National Statistics

To make real progress, and to encourage everyone to take part, four national targets have been set for improving health by the year 2010.

- **Heart disease and stroke:** to reduce the death rate from heart disease and stroke and related illnesses amongst people aged 65 years by at least a **further third** than in the Health of the Nation document.
- **Accidents:** to reduce accidents by at least a further **fifth**.
- **Cancer:** to reduce the death rate from cancer amongst people aged under 65 years by at least a further **fifth**.
- **Mental health:** to reduce the death rate from suicide and undetermined injury by at least a further **sixth**.

Build your learning

Summary points

- Health can be defined in different ways. A negative approach is based on the absence, or lack, of illness. A positive approach involves identifying some of the qualities and abilities of a healthy person.

- In defining health and well-being it is important to consider an individual's physical, social, intellectual, emotional, psychological and mental health.

- The term well-being refers to the way people feel about themselves. Having friends, feeling confident, being in control and having access to food, warmth and shelter are important factors in well-being.

- Disease is the term used to describe physical changes that are damaging to the correct structure or functioning of a person's body.

- The government has defined targets for health in *The Health of the Nation* and *Our Healthier Nation*. These involve reducing levels of particular diseases and health problems.

- *Our Healthier Nation* is a document that sets out plans to improve the health of the worst off in society and the least healthy neighbourhoods.

- The most important areas for improvement that are identified are coronary heart disease and stroke, cancers, accidents and mental illness.

Key words and phrases

You should know the meaning of the words and phrases listed below as they relate to ideas about health. If you are not sure about any of them, go back through the last 11 pages to check or refresh your understanding.

- Physical health
- Mental health
- Social health
- Disease

- Intellectual health
- Well-being
- Emotional health
- Psychological health

- Health promotion
- *The Health of the Nation*
- *Our Healthier Nation*
- Holistic approach

Student questions

1 Explain the difference in meaning between health and well-being.

2 Name two different ways in which health can be defined.

3 What does psychological health involve?

4 What did *The Health of the Nation* identify and set out to achieve?

5 Which groups did the government aim to help through the health promotion strategy it set out in *Our Healthier Nation*?

6 Name the key areas for improvement of health which are identified in *Our Healthier Nation*.

7 How does the World Health Organisation define health?

Changing health needs across the life span

In this section we look at the idea of health needs and consider how people's needs change over their lifetime. An understanding of health needs, and the ways in which these change over time, will help you later when you are asked to plan some health targets for an individual.

In order to experience health and a positive feeling of well-being an individual must meet, and be able to balance, his or her physical, social, emotional and intellectual needs at any point in time.

- Physical needs involve all the physical and material things that a person should have in order to be healthy. They include food, clothing, shelter, warmth, diet, rest, exercise, personal hygiene and cleanliness.
- Social needs include all the things that enable a person to enjoy relationships with others. For example, an appropriate environment, education, involvement with other people, friends, opportunities to join social groups and organisations, and to be employed.
- Intellectual needs include a suitable and safe environment where an individual's mental capacity and natural abilities can be developed from a very early age. It covers, for example, mental stimulation, education, and employment.
- Emotional needs include a feeling of security, enjoyment of life, happiness, love and contentment. People often try to avoid unpleasant emotions such as worry, loneliness and grief.
- Mental health needs involve having the necessary support network in times of difficulty, anxiety, and depression, particularly after an event such as bereavement, which causes distress. In mental illness, these feelings, which are normal after a distressing event, occur to a much greater extent and last for a longer period of time, making it difficult for a person to cope.

The health and well-being needs of different groups

Despite the fact that no two individuals are exactly the same, it is likely that people in the same life stage (see page 162) will have some shared health needs. In particular, they will have similar physical health needs. Some of these shared needs are identified in the sections that follow. However, even when individuals have common physical health needs, they can have different social, emotional, and intellectual well-being needs. It is always important to try to understand what a person's particular, individual needs are in order to help them to achieve maximum health and well-being. In this section we outline some general health and well-being needs associated with different life stages.

The needs of babies and infants (0–3 years)

Babies and infants have certain basic health needs. Some of these are essential for the baby to survive and to grow and develop physically. Others provide favourable conditions for social, intellectual and emotional development. The needs of babies and infants include:

- warmth, food, clothing, shelter, fresh air and sunlight
- activity and rest, love and comfort,
- security and a sense of safety
- protection from illness and injury
- secure attachments and continuity of care
- training in good habits and skills
- opportunities to develop trust
- praise and understanding to develop self-confidence
- stimulation from play to assist learning.

The needs of young children (3–9 years)

As the child grows older, there are increased and additional needs. These include:

- companions and friends to play with
- opportunities to explore surroundings
- opportunities to become independent
- opportunities to be helpful to others in the home, at school and at play
- opportunities to develop intelligence, be successful and achieve
- opportunities to take responsibility
- opportunities to develop self-control
- discipline which is firm but kind
- praise and positive criticism.

The needs of adolescents (10–18 years)

Adolescence is a period in life in which great changes occur as the person approaches adulthood. It is a period of transition, during which time puberty begins, the stage at which a person's reproductive or sex organs become able to function. At this time, girls start having periods or menstruating. Some girls start this process at a very early age while others are quite late in starting. No one knows exactly when puberty will start or how long it will take to complete.

The onset of puberty can be a time of confusion for adolescents and may result in emotional stress which is sometimes misinterpreted by adults. It is a time when parents need all their skill, imagination and patience if they and their children are to emerge at the end with affection and respect for one another. The social and emotional needs of adolescents include:

- respect for their opinions so they can build up a working knowledge of themselves and their judgements
- love and security expressed in a different way from that of the child
- opportunities to develop self-control
- opportunities for self-development and attainment of skills
- situations in which to test themselves
- opportunities to socialise and develop a sense of identity
- confidence in themselves and their achievements
- training for adult roles and responsibilities
- advice about relationships, sex and sexuality.

Adults (19–65 years)
The social and emotional needs of adults vary considerably. They include:

- awareness of self
- stable relationships
- job security and work ethics
- development of a sense of achievement and purpose
- development of skills and interests
- opportunities to develop self
- leisure activities and free time
- advice and information about health issues, groups and organisations
- preparation and advice for retirement.

Pregnant women
Pregnant women experience a lot of changes, both physically and emotionally. As pregnancy progresses and the fetus (unborn child) grows, the woman increases in physical size. Feelings and moods may alter at various stages in the pregnancy because of the hormonal changes that are taking place in the body. Large amounts of hormones – oestrogens and progesterones – are secreted by the placenta, the tissue from which the fetus gets its nourishment.

While some women are excited at the prospect of the birth of their baby, others may have more negative experiences. Some women experience anxiety about the pregnancy and many feel apprehensive about whether the baby is developing normally. As the pregnancy progresses, some women become

▼ Health care information for pregnant women

Pregnant?

Eating and Drinking During Pregnancy

98

quite tired. All these changes can cause mood swings, so that the woman is sometimes very happy and at other times weepy. Throughout the pregnancy the woman needs:

- professional advice and encouragement
- love, affection and support from partners, relatives and friends
- advice on community health service facilities and provisions
- proper nutrition in adequate quantities
- exercise, rest and leisure activities
- opportunities to develop a positive attitude towards parenting.

Elderly people (over 65 years)

A number of physical, social, emotional and intellectual changes occur in midlife and old age. These are life stages when children are leaving, or have left, home and couples are able to spend more time together, perhaps travelling and doing things they could not have done when they were working full time.

When people retire from full-time employment, they lose their work role and contact with work colleagues and experience a drop in income. The changes that occur as they enter old age can be overwhelming for some people, although many manage the necessary adjustments and find new experiences to enjoy. However, some people experience an inactive retirement because of illness, immobility, incontinence or intellectual impairment. In order to be healthy in old age people need:

- respect from others
- to be valued by society
- general care and attention
- safe, comfortable familiar surroundings
- adequate finances and security
- community health facilities and resources
- supportive and stimulating relationships
- practical help and support to adjust to loss
- activity and rest
- leisure activities.

Minority groups

The United Kingdom is a multicultural society. It now consists of people of many different nationalities and backgrounds. They make up different communities, dependent on their ethnic origins, religion, culture, beliefs and traditions. The

▲ Old age can be a time for trying new experiences

cultural needs, attitudes and values and behaviours of people in the United Kingdom are diverse and should be respected. For example, African and Caribbean people have a different culture, and different cultural needs, from Chinese people and people from the different Asian communities.

Different groups behave in different ways. They behave differently when they greet each other, show courtesy or observe their religion, for example. Jehovah's Witnesses follow a form of religion which involves specific restrictions regarding their health needs. In particular, they do not have blood transfusions because of their religious beliefs. It is therefore important to take into account people's cultural and religious needs regarding opportunities to:

- worship and follow their own religious faith
- socialise within their own communities
- maintain cultural values, beliefs and traditions
- be free from prejudice and discrimination
- progress like any other member of society
- live peacefully within the wider society
- access education, employment and housing.

Homeless people

Adequate housing is a basic necessity. However, a large number of individuals of all ages, but particularly young people, are homeless and lack adequate shelter. Homelessness has a direct adverse effect on health and well-being. Homeless people are more at risk of contracting infections such as tuberculosis and HIV, have higher rates of alcohol and drug addiction and are vulnerable to becoming victims of crime and exploitation. In terms of health and well-being, homeless people need to be:

- valued by society
- treated with respect by the wider society
- helped to find adequate shelter, food and warmth
- given information on how their needs can be met
- referred to the appropriate agencies for advice and support
- encouraged to use health and community preventive services.

Travellers

Travellers have a nomadic lifestyle. They move around in small communities, living in caravans and converted vehicles, usually on campsites. Statutory education and health facilities that are provided by the NHS and local authorities are often not taken up by travellers. This is mainly because they do not remain in

◄ Travellers can find statutory
health care and education
services hard to access

one area for very long, but also because they find services hard
to access. The needs of travellers are different from those of
other groups. They include the need for:

- help and support to maintain a reasonable standard of life
- encouragement to use the health facilities and services
  generally provided
- appropriate community health preventive services
- appropriate education services
- respect and acceptance of their values and way of life so
  that they can live without hindrance or harassment and free
  from prejudice and discrimination.

People with special needs

Special needs is a broad term which embraces a variety of
disabling conditions. These are mainly inherited or acquired
conditions that affect health and well-being. Irrespective of the
particular conditions that people with special needs may have,
they are likely to have additional needs, including:

- appropriate facilities and resources to maintain well-being
- understanding and tolerance from society
- professional advice and support
- practical help and support
- support to enable them to live healthy and independent lives
- suitably adapted premises
- accessible local services such as schools and libraries
- opportunities to continue further training and education
- suitable employment
- opportunities to interact and socialise with other groups
- opportunities and facilities for leisure and sport.

Build your learning

Summary points

- When considering the needs of various people and groups it is important to consider their physical health and social, emotional and intellectual well-being.

- People who belong to the same social groups (for example travellers) and those who are in the same life stage (for example, children or older people) tend to have some general, shared physical health needs.

- Health and well-being needs change throughout the life span and vary between different social groups.

- It is always important to assess an individual's particular health and well-being needs rather than assume that they will always be the same as those of people with similar social and physical characteristics.

Key words and phrases

You should know the meaning of the words and phrases listed below as they relate to aspects of the health and well-being of different people and groups in society.

- **Physical needs**
- **Social needs**
- **Intellectual needs**
- **Emotional needs**
- **Life stage**
- **Puberty**
- **Fetus**
- **Placenta**

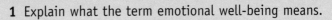

Student questions

1 Explain what the term emotional well-being means.

2 List five things that all people require in order to meet their physical health needs.

3 Which health need areas might be affected when a person retires from work?

4 Give two examples of how people's culture affects their health and well-being needs.

5 Explain why homeless people have lifestyles that sometimes mean that they are unable to meet their health and well-being needs.

Factors affecting health and well-being

Your health and well-being is influenced and affected by a number of physical, social and economic factors. Good health and well-being are more likely to be experienced by people who manage to achieve a balanced lifestyle and who have a secure and sustainable environment. In the next section we will explore examples of each of these factors.

Dietary factors

The term **diet** refers to the type and amount of food regularly eaten and drunk. Eating a varied and adequate diet on a daily basis is part of the process of achieving good personal health.

◄ A balanced diet

A balanced diet is one that contains suitable amounts of each of the five basic nutrients. These are carbohydrates, fats, proteins, vitamins, and minerals. **Nutrients** are naturally occurring chemical substances found in different foods. They perform one or more of three functions:

- providing materials for building, repairing and maintaining body tissues
- helping to regulate body processes
- serving as fuel to provide energy.

Carbohydrates

Carbohydrates provide the body with energy. They are found in a large group of foodstuffs which include sugars, starches and fibre. There are two main types of carbohydrate. The first type consists of foods containing sugar and sugar sources, such as jam, cakes and biscuits which provide the body with energy (in calories) but not with useful nutrients. The second type consists of starchy foods such as potatoes, rice and pasta which provide the body with a rich source of energy.

▼ Foods containing saturated and unsaturated fats

Fats

Fats also provide the body with energy but they have a much higher energy value than carbohydrates. There are two main types of fats, saturated and unsaturated.

Saturated fats can be found in animal and vegetable sources. Animal fats are found in beef, lamb, pork, lard and dripping and in dairy products such as milk, butter and cheese. Vegetable fats are present in foods such as coconut oil and chocolate. It is important to limit the intake of saturated fats as they contain a high level of cholesterol. This is responsible for coronary heart disease by causing the arteries to narrow. In 1998, coronary heart disease was responsible for 121,037 deaths in England and Wales.

Unsaturated fats are found in vegetable oils and products such as sunflower, corn or soya oils, special soft margarine, nuts, and oily fish such as herring. Included in these unsaturated fats are a special group called polyunsaturated fats or polyunsaturates. Unsaturated fats do not raise cholesterol in the same way as saturates. Our bodies need a small amount of polyunsaturated fats to help make and repair body cells.

Proteins

Proteins provide the chemical substances needed to build and repair cells and tissues in the body. They are particularly important in childhood for building the brain, muscles, skin, blood and other tissues. Proteins are the building blocks of all human tissues. They are made up of amino acids. An adult needs 21 different amino acids but the body can only make twelve of them. The other nine come from the food we eat.

There are two kinds of protein. Animal protein contains all nine essential amino acids. Sources of animal protein include lean meat, fish, egg white, milk and cheese. Vegetable proteins do not contain all the essential amino acids. Sources of vegetable protein include foods such as lentils, baked beans and soya beans. These contain a high level of amino acids and are a good source of protein for those on vegetarian diets.

Vitamins

Vitamins help to regulate the chemical reactions that are continuously taking place in our bodies. They are found in most of the food that we eat. They are protective substances that combine with other chemicals to form enzymes. Enzymes cause chemical activities to take place. The body only requires a small quantity of each vitamin to keep it healthy and active. The human body cannot manufacture its own vitamins. A lack of any of them can result in deficiency diseases.

Figure 2.3: Characteristics of common vitamins

Name	Function	Sources	Deficiency effects
A (Retinol)	Prevents infection, keeps skin and bones healthy, helps with night vision.	Cheese, butter, oily fish, milk, carrots, spinach.	Inability to see in the dark. Dry, patchy skin. Unhealthy mucus membrane.
B_1 (Thiamine)	Needed for energy production in cells. Helps growth and repair of body tissues.	Breakfast cereal, brown rice, nuts, wholemeal bread, eggs, fish, pork, liver, kidney, beans.	Muscle weakness, skin problems, nervous disorders, beri-beri.
B_{12}	Helps in the production of red blood cells. Helps growth.	Kidney, chicken, beef, pork, dairy products.	Anaemia, sore mouth and tongue, spinal cord damage.
C (Ascorbic acid)	Aids the healing of wounds and fractures. Keeps gums and teeth healthy. Protects against coughs and colds.	Fresh fruit and vegetables, especially citrus fruits.	Scurvy, slow healing of wounds and fractures.
D	Needed for strong bones and teeth. Aids the absorption of minerals.	Foods containing fat, such as margarine, butter, oily fish and eggs.	Rickets in children, soft bones and muscle weakness in adults.
E	Needed to keep the skin supple and elastic.	Vegetable oils, wholemeal bread, rice, eggs, butter, green leaf vegetables.	Not yet known.
K	Needed to promote clotting of the blood when bleeding.	Liver, fresh green vegetables.	Bleeding under the skin. Blood slow to clot.

Minerals

Minerals are basic chemical elements, like calcium and iron, which are found naturally in the soil and the air. Minerals are essential to life. They are needed to build and repair certain tissues and for control of body function. Some minerals, such as calcium, phosphorous, potassium, sodium and iron, are needed by the body in large quantities. Others, such as zinc and iodine, are needed in much smaller quantities. People get their mineral intake by:

- eating vegetables which have absorbed minerals from the soil
- eating the meat of animals which have themselves eaten mineral-rich plants
- drinking water in which minerals are dissolved.

Calcium is a mineral that is essential for strong bones and teeth, muscle contraction and maintenance of body fluids. Sources of calcium include milk, cheese, white bread, yoghurt, ice-cream, and green vegetables. People who do not have sufficient calcium may develop weak bones.

Iron is essential for the production of haemoglobin in red blood cells. Sources of iron include red meat, egg yolk, green vegetables, liver, wholemeal bread, some breakfast cereals and potatoes. People who does not have enough iron in their diet may develop anaemia.

Fluoride is a mineral that helps to produce strong healthy teeth. It has been added to the water supply in some parts of the United Kingdom and is an ingredient of toothpaste. A deficiency of fluoride can lead to mottling of the teeth and tooth decay.

In 1991, the Committee on Medical Aspects of Food Policy (COMA), which was set up by the Department of Health, produced a report on dietary reference values (DRVs) for food, energy and nutrients for the United Kingdom. This report provided a firm scientific basis for dietary advice to the public. It deals with the broad range of dietary requirements for all groups of individuals within the population. It sets out the reference nutrient intake (RNI) of vitamins and minerals for different groups of people, with figures for different age groups, men and women, and advice for pregnant and breast-feeding women. Figures 2.4 and 2.5 show the reference nutrient intakes of some minerals and vitamins for selected groups of people.

Taking extra vitamin tablets to supplement a person's natural dietary vitamin intake has become a commonly accepted, though often unnecessary, way of reducing the risk of certain illnesses or boosting health. For example, it is not necessary for women who are, or who might become, pregnant to take supplements containing vitamin A, unless advised to do so by their GP or antenatal clinic. They should not eat liver because of the high content of vitamin A.

There is no need for supplements of vitamin D to be taken by adults provided that the skin is sufficiently exposed to the sun. For those who do not go out in the sun very much, such as some elderly people, or others who wear a particular form of dress because of their traditions or religion (such as some Muslims and some people from the Asian subcontinent) an additional supply is needed. In order to prevent vitamin D deficiency in infants and young children, the government recommended that all babies and children should be given vitamin drops up to the age of five.

Figure 2.4: Reference nutrient intake (RNI) for selected minerals

Group	Age range	Calcium mg/day	Phosporus mg/day	Magnesium mg/day	Sodium mg/day	Potassium mg/day	Chloride mg/day	Iron mg/day
Babies	0–3 months	525	400	55	210	800	320	1.7
Children	4–6 years	450	350	120	700	1,100	1,100	6.1
Males	15–18 years	1,000	775	300	1,600	3,500	2,500	11.3
Males	19–50 years	700	550	300	1,600	3,500	2,500	8.7
Women	15–18 years	800	625	300	1,600	3,500	2,500	14.8
Women	19–50 years	700	550	270	1,600	3,500	2,500	14.8

Figure 2.5: Reference nutrient intake (RNI) for selected vitamins

Group	Age range	Vitamin B_1 mg/day	Vitamin B_{12} mg/day	Folate µg/day	Vitamin C mg/day	Vitamin A µg/day	Vitamin D µg/day
Babies	0–3 months	0.2	0.3	50	25	350	8.5
Children	4–6 years	0.7	0.8	100	30	500	–
Males	15–18 years	1.1	1.5	200	40	700	–
Males	19–50 years	1.0	1.5	200	40	700	–
Women	15–18 years	0.8	1.5	200	40	600	–
Women	19–50 years	0.8	1.5	200	40	600	–

Fibre and water

Fibre and water are also very important constituents of the food that we eat but are not counted as nutrients. Dietary fibre adds bulk to food and encourages the muscular movement (peristalsis) of food through the digestive system and intestines. Fibre is found in vegetables, fruit, wholemeal bread; in pulses, such as peas and beans; and in cereals, such as oats, rice and bran. Lack of fibre in the diet can result in constipation and poor digestion of food.

Water is essential to life. About 80 per cent of the weight of a newborn child is made up of water. In adulthood, water accounts for 75 per cent of body weight. Water is the main component of body cells and blood. It also helps to moisten and lubricate the lining of joints. Lack of water leads to dehydration and death.

ACTIVITY

Nutritional diets?

Figure 2.6 is a diet record sheet showing the weekend food consumption of the members of the O'Brien family. Use the sheet to answer these questions.

1 Indicate which nutrients are contained in the foods eaten by the family.

2 Identify the effect of each nutrient on the body.

3 How nutritional is the diet of this family?

4 Do you think that individual family members are getting a balanced diet?

5 Are there any deficiencies or excesses in their nutritional intakes?

Using examples from the record sheet, write a paragraph explaining your views on the last three questions. What advice would you give to the parents of Brendan and Emma about the type of diet needed to promote healthy growth and development in children? You might want to read the next section on individual nutritional needs before answering this question.

You discover more about the O'Brien family in Unit 3.

Figure 2.6: Diet record sheet for the O'Brien family

Family member	Day	Breakfast	Lunch	Snacks	Evening meal
Gerry age 40	Sat	Boiled egg, toast, coffee	Ham roll, crisps, coffee	Doughnut, coffee	Pizza, salad, baked potatoes, beer, chocolate cake
	Sun	Fried egg, bacon, toast, coffee	Roast chicken, roast potatoes, peas, carrots, tinned fruit, ice cream, wine, coffee	Chocolate bar, coffee	Cheese and pickle sandwich, fruit cake, tea
Fiona age 30	Sat	Boiled egg, toast, tea	Crispbread, cottage cheese, herb tea	Apple, diet coke	Pizza, salad, diet coke, orange, coffee
	Sun	Toast, marmalade, orange juice, tea	Roast chicken, peas, carrots, ice cream, wine, coffee	Banana, diet coke	Fruit cake, tea
Emma age 8	Sat	Cornflakes, orange juice	Ham roll, crisps, blackcurrant squash	Chocolate bar, cola drink	Pizza, salad, baked potato, blackcurrant squash, chocolate cake
	Sun	Fried egg, toast, orange juice	Roast chicken, roast potatoes, carrots, ice cream, wafers, grape juice	Chocolate milkshake	Cheese sandwich, sponge cake, milk
Brendan age 3	Sat	Ready Brek, milk	Tuna sandwich, apple, orange juice	Chocolate bar, milk	Pizza, salad, blackcurrant squash, chocolate cake
	Sun	Toast, Marmite, milk	Roast chicken, roast potato, peas, ice cream, wafers, grape juice	Chocolate milkshake	Fruit yoghurt, sponge cake, blackcurrant squash
Sarah age 73	Sat	Grapefruit, crispbread, marmalade, tea	Roll, cottage cheese, tomato, herb tea	Apple	Pizza, salad, chocolate cake, tea
	Sun	Boiled egg, toast, tea	Roast chicken, roast potato, peas, carrots, tinned fruit, ice cream, wine, coffee	Nothing	Tuna sandwich, fruit cake, tea

Individual nutritional needs

Every individual needs food in sufficient quantities to survive. It is a basic and fundamental human need. A lack of nutritious food over a period of time can adversely affect health and physical performance. The amount of nutritious food needed varies from person to person. It is dependent upon:

- age
- gender
- body size
- height
- weight
- the physical and climatic conditions, for example, whether it is a cold or a warm country
- whether the person is living an active life or one that is not physically active (a sedentary life).

For example:

- babies and infants need suitable nutrition in adequate quantities to enable them to grow and develop normally and to prevent certain minor illnesses
- young children need greater amounts of some nutrients than their size would indicate, because they are growing
- adolescents need adequate nutrients in quantities that maintain their growth and sustain their physical activities
- pregnant women need extra energy and increased amounts of certain nutrients to nourish themselves and their baby
- older women might need to take extra supplements of oestrogens and regular exercise or physical activity to prevent and avoid the risk of osteoporosis, a painful arthritic condition which affects the larger and weight-bearing bones in the body
- people exposed to cold weather must have additional nutrients because the body uses more energy to stay at the same temperature
- men need more calories to keep their tissues healthy as their bodies have a greater percentage of muscle tissue than a women's bodies.

Some groups of people have special diets. These require them to leave out or include specific food groups to meet their personal values or special physical needs.

Vegetarians do not eat meat or fish. They can still obtain all their nutrients from a diet containing no meat. Their proteins can be obtained from cereals, beans, eggs and cheese. Vegans, who eat no animal products at all, can obtain all the essential nutrients provided their vegetarian diet is varied. Pregnant or nursing mothers must eat and drink sensibly in order to provide adequate nutrition and fluids for themselves and for their children.

Planning nutritious diets

Plan a week's menu of nutritious, balanced meals for each of the following people.

- A woman in the first three months (first trimester) of pregnancy. You should include sources of all the necessary nutrients that make up a balanced diet.

- An infant aged six months to one year. Include breakfast, mid-morning snack, lunch, tea and supper.

- A toddler of 18 months to two years. Include breakfast, mid-morning snack, lunch, tea and supper.

- A male teenager, aged 15 years, who takes part in a lot of sports activity.

- A woman aged 26 who is the practice manager of a busy firm of city solicitors.

- An elderly man who has walking difficulties but who is able to move slowly around his home.

Exercise and recreation

Physical activity contributes to good general health and well-being. In order to achieve maximum health benefits from physical activity, exercise needs to be undertaken regularly. Exercise contributes to health in different ways. The type and level of exercise individuals do depends on their age, gender, and other physical factors. Moderate exercise can be undertaken by older, and less physically mobile people, including pregnant women in the later stages of pregnancy, or by people with disabilities. More vigorous and energetic exercise is undertaken by younger people, and by people who are more physically able.

There are also many significant psychological benefits to be gained from exercise and recreation. For example, regular exercise helps to build confidence and self-esteem and gives a general feeling of well-being.

Exercise has many health benefits as it:

- is great fun and a good way of socialising
- enables the individual to feel more energetic
- helps relaxation and reduces or relieves stress
- increases stamina for daily living
- helps to control and maintain a healthy body weight
- improves the ability of skeletal muscles to extract oxygen from the blood, reducing the demand for blood flow
- reduces the risk of heart attacks
- strengthens muscles, joints and bones
- improves the staying power of muscles
- helps the heart to work more efficiently
- improves circulation and reduces the risk of heart disease
- increases suppleness and mobility as the body ages.

▲ Working out

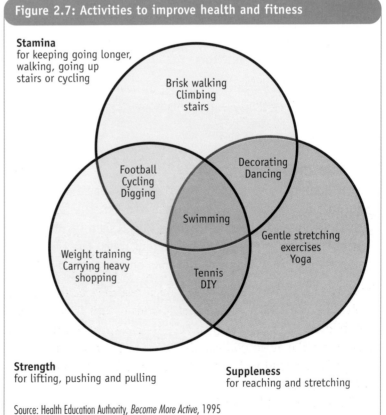

Figure 2.7: Activities to improve health and fitness

Stamina
for keeping going longer, walking, going up stairs or cycling

Brisk walking
Climbing stairs

Football
Cycling
Digging

Decorating
Dancing

Swimming

Weight training
Carrying heavy shopping

Tennis
DIY

Gentle stretching exercises
Yoga

Strength
for lifting, pushing and pulling

Suppleness
for reaching and stretching

Source: Health Education Authority, *Become More Active*, 1995

Figure 2.8: The health benefits of different activities

Activity	Stamina	Muscular/ Strength	Suppleness flexibility	Coordination
Aerobics	*****	**	**	****
Badminton	***	***	****	*****
Bowls	*	**	***	***
Cricket	**	*****	**	****
Cycling*	*****	*****	**	****
Dancing	****	*****	****	*****
Fitness class	****	*****	****	****
Football	****	*****	****	****
Gardening	***	****	**	***
Golf	**	**	***	****
Hill walking	***	**	*	**
Horse riding	*	****	*	****
Jogging	****	****	**	**
Netball	***	****	****	*****
Rowing*	*****	*****	**	****
Running	*****	*****	**	**
Squash	****	****	****	*****
Stair climbing	****	***	*	**
Swimming*	*****	*****	*****	*****
Tennis	***	****	****	*****
Walking briskly	***	**	*	*
Weight training	**	*****	*	****
Yoga	*	**	*****	***

*	no real effect
**	beneficial effect
***	good effect
****	very good effect
*****	excellent effect

*energetically

Source: Health Education Authority, *Becoming More Active*, 1995

Rest and sleep

People need to rest every day to maintain their health and well-being. Babies, young children, older people and pregnant women tend to require a period of rest during the day. Most healthy adults and older children need rest only at the end of their active day. At nurseries and toddler groups it is routine for children to have a sleep to help them to feel refreshed and relaxed for the afternoon activities. Some older people are less energetic and tend to feel tired more quickly than teenagers and younger adults.

There are two different kinds of sleep. Non-rapid eye movement sleep occurs when a person first falls asleep.

Activity decreases and the muscles are greatly but not completely relaxed. The heartbeat and breathing slow down and the eyelids remain quite still. The depth of sleep then increases. Rapid eye movement sleep occurs when the person's eyes move jerkily under their closed lids. The heart and breathing rates quicken and the muscles, particularly in the neck, are completely relaxed. This is the sleep in which dreaming occurs.

On going to bed, drowsiness is followed by non-rapid eye movement sleep. After about 90 minutes rapid eye movement sleep occurs.

Sleep patterns

Sleep patterns develop gradually. Newborn babies sleep for brief periods throughout the day and night. By the age of three months, most babies have learned to sleep through the night. By the age of six, most children will have given up daytime sleep. The amount of sleep required varies according to age. A four-year-old child sleeps an average of ten to fourteen hours a day, and a ten-year-old about nine to twelve hours. Most adults sleep from seven to eight and a half hours every night. Others require as few as four or five hours or as many as ten hours each night. Most people find that they need slightly less sleep as they grow older. A person who slept eight hours a night at age thirty may need only six or seven hours when he or she is sixty years old.

People deprived of sleep lose energy and become quick-tempered. After two days without sleep, lengthy concentration becomes difficult. Through pure determination people may perform tasks well for short periods, but they will be easily distracted. Other negative effects of sleep loss include:

- mistakes in routine tasks
- slips of attention
- dozing off for periods of a few seconds or more
- falling asleep completely
- difficulty seeing and hearing clearly
- confusion.

Environment

The environment in which people live is an important factor affecting their ability to maintain health and well-being. The way in which the environment affects our health is complex. We all need things such as clean air and water, proper waste disposal facilities and good quality housing.

Other environmental factors that affect health and well-

◀ Air pollution from traffic is a common problem for city dwellers

being include where we live, the amount of money we have and what we do for a living. Many of the factors which affect our health are beyond our control. For example, when it comes to buying food we can choose what we think is best for us from what is available and affordable, but we cannot, in many cases, do anything about where we work, or clean up the air we breathe. Such changes can be brought about, however, by education and group action from committed individuals in the community.

A healthy environment and clean surroundings can enhance people's outlook on life and the way they feel about themselves. You will find that certain illnesses affect groups of people who live in the same area, or who do the same type of job, or who have the same lifestyle. While the incidence of a particular illness in an area may be explained to a large extent by the characteristics of the resident population, in terms of age, sex and physical condition, the main cause may lie in the environment in which they live. Recent studies suggest that high levels of ozone in the air in the summer months leads to increased hospital admissions for respiratory conditions such as asthma.

Social class

Studies have shown that health and illness are linked to social class. One way of defining social class is by grouping people according to their occupation. This is known as the Registrar General's scale of social class (see Figure 2.9). The classification has been used to assess whether there is a link between health and a person's position in society.

Studies have shown that, the higher a person's social class, the more likely he or she is to achieve and enjoy good health.

People in the higher social classes seem to have lower mortality (death) rates in any given year. Illnesses, infections, some accidents and diseases related to poor living situations, and poverty, contribute to higher mortality and are more likely to be experienced by people in the lower class groups.

Figure 2.9: The Register General's scale of social class

Social class	Category	Examples
I	Professional	Surveyor, lawyer
II	Intermediate/ managerial	Musician, farmer
III Non-manual	Skilled non-manual	Clerical worker
III Manual	Skilled manual	Bricklayer, driver
IV	Partly skilled	Barperson, gardener
V	Unskilled	Labourer

Figure 2.10: Infant mortality by social class

	Rates per 1,000 live births	
	1981	1996
Professional	7.8	3.6
Managerial	8.2	4.4
Skilled non-manual	9.0	5.4
Skilled manual	10.5	5.8
Partly skilled	12.7	5.9
Unskilled	15.7	7.8
Other	15.6	8.3
All	10.4	5.4

Notes: Figures record deaths of babies within one year of birth in the United Kingdom. Social class is based on the occupation of the father.

Source: Office for National Statistics, General Registrar Office for Scotland, Northern Ireland Statistics and Research Agency

Housing

The type of housing in which people live can also have a positive or negative effect on health and well-being. If a person's home is overcrowded, damp and cold, or carries a fire hazard or an accident risk then it is likely to have a negative impact on health. Indeed, in many cases it may be the cause of the person's ill health. Cold and damp housing can aggravate many medical conditions, in particular, asthma, bronchitis and other respiratory diseases, rheumatism and arthritis. These conditions affect all ages but are particularly unpleasant for babies, infants and older people. Overcrowding encourages the spread of infection and infectious diseases such as tuberculosis and dysentery and accidents are more likely to happen to children who live in overcrowded homes. Sleeplessness and stress are also associated with overcrowding.

People living in high-rise tower blocks or bedsits can suffer from social isolation because of the nature of their housing. This in turn can lead to depression and low self-esteem. High-rise blocks of flats were built in the United Kingdom during the 1950s and 1960s when there was acute housing need. The government's long-term plan is now to gradually phase these buildings out and replace them with more suitable housing that will appeal to the wider community. Today, many new housing blocks do not extend beyond four floors.

▲ Tower blocks are gradually being replaced by low-rise housing

Education

People's educational achievements affect their outlook on life and, indirectly, their health and well-being. Educational achievement plays an important part in the type of occupation that a person chooses and has access to. Occupation determines people's earnings and their ability to afford good quality housing and holidays. Education may also play a role in enabling people to access health and social care services. Good all-round education appears to have a positive impact on the life chances and the health outcomes of the individual.

Employment

Work is a very important factor in the well-being of the individual. An employed person uses the skills, knowledge and expertise which he or she has already gained and has the opportunity to acquire new skills. Apart from being gainfully employed and earning, work provides an opportunity to socialise and to keep in contact with society. Work provides security, both financially and socially, as well as social stimulation. An employed person has a routine and a pattern to the day. Work gives status, confidence and self-respect.

However, if the person becomes unemployed, all this is lost and the result can adversely affect the health and well-being of the individual and his or her family with quite devastating consequences. This is the case for many families, but worse in households where one adult may be bringing up children on his or her own. Life can be very difficult both financially and socially as a result of unemployment.

A person who is not working may suffer from lack of security, both financially and socially. There might be mental symptoms and stress which causes psychological and mental misery such as depression, anxiety, worry for oneself and the family, as well as unhappiness, dissatisfaction, lack of confidence, low self-esteem and difficulty in sleeping. The psychological and mental health damage can last for a very long period or until the person regains employment and some degree of job satisfaction. Official figures published in April 1999 show the number of people unemployed at 1.3 million.

Income

The amount of money people earn can determine their whole lifestyle. People with more money generally have better housing, and may eat a more balanced diet. Money can also mean having good and frequent holidays, warm clothing and private transport. The poorer the person, or the less adequate the means, the less likely he or she will be to make use of the National Health Service and community health facilities, even though he or she might have worse or failing health.

One of the ways in which people can influence their income is by changing jobs, achieving promotion, or obtaining a pay rise. This depends on the person's level of education and degree of qualification or skills. We all know that education is not the only avenue by which an individual can obtain a high wage or income. Many sports personalities, entertainment artists and entrepreneurs have amassed huge fortunes by using their talents. However, the vast majority of people present a picture of achievement through hard work, ability, and self-belief.

For some people, however, achieving might be difficult for a whole range of reasons. They may therefore have to resort to public funds because they are unable to gain employment. Social security benefits are provided by the State to help to improve the standard of living for people who are in need. Many people are entitled to benefits because they are unable to work, have been made redundant, have special needs, or are seeking employment.

Build your learning

Summary points

- Diet, exercise and sleep are important influences on an individual's physical health.

- A number of social and economic factors including social class, the environment, employment, housing, education and income also have an effect on the health and well-being of the individual.

- These factors affect people in different ways, such as whether they are able to access appropriate health care services and facilities, and housing needs.

- People from the higher social classes are likely to live longer and their survival rates for cancer are much higher.

- People in the lower social classes are more likely to die younger from diseases such as cancer, from accidents and from smoking related diseases.

- People who live in overcrowded conditions are more likely to suffer from stress, social isolation, depression, and low self-esteem.

- Cold, damp housing conditions also contribute to ill health, especially asthma, bronchitis, rheumatism, and arthritis.

Key words and phrases

You should know the meaning of the words and phrases listed below, as they relate to the factors that contribute to health and well-being. If you are not sure about any of them, go back through the last 16 pages to check or refresh your understanding.

- **Peristalsis**
- **Mortality**
- **Unsaturated fats**
- **Nutrient**
- **Diet**
- **Animal protein**
- **Vegetable protein**
- **Asthma**
- **Saturated fats**
- **Bronchitis**
- **Osteoporosis**
- **Rheumatism**
- **Arthritis**
- **Mortality**

Student questions

1 Describe some of the ways in which a person's housing situation can affect his or her health and well-being.

2 In what ways can employment contribute to a person's well-being?

3 How can unemployment affect the social, psychological and physical health of the individual and his or her family?

4 In your own words, explain how social class is related to health.

5 Which social class would a doctor, a qualified nurse and a hospital porter be in according to the Registrar General's classification of social class?

6 Make a list of the different health problems that can result from poor housing.

Risks to health

In the last section we considered how physical, social and economic factors can enable people to experience positive health and well-being. In this section we are going to look at the other side of the health behaviour coin. Some types of lifestyle and behaviour are known to put health and well-being at risk. For example, alcohol and tobacco are two widely available substances that can cause health problems and dependency if misused. Because of the evidence linking the use of both these substances to ill health and disease, they can only be bought legally by adults. Illegal drugs such as cocaine and heroin can also have a negative effect on health. Similarly, lack of exercise or a poor diet can make ill health more likely.

Drug use and misuse

Drugs are chemical substances that affect the body's chemistry and functioning. They are widely used and available in the United Kingdom. They can be obtained by:

- doctor's prescription – drugs used for medical treatment
- purchase over the counter – medicinal drugs (from a chemist) or legal substances such as alcohol and tobacco
- illegal purchase – controlled drugs or non-prescribed medicinal drugs.

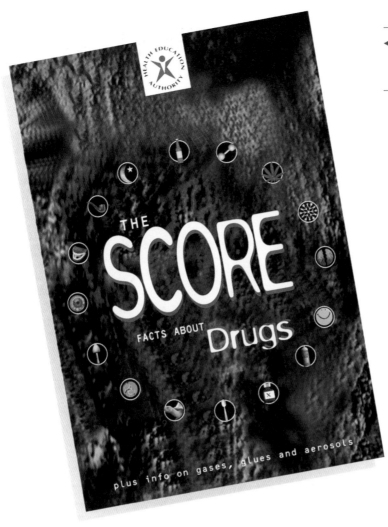

A government information booklet about drugs and drugs use

Misuse of drugs intended for medical treatment

Some of the medical profession's most valuable tools are the drugs that have been developed to treat specific illnesses and diseases. Many of these drugs can only be legally prescribed and used by doctors in medical situations. Other, over-the-counter drugs may be purchased without a doctor's permission.

Some drugs that are intended for specific medical use are frequently misused. These drugs may be obtained legally, on prescription, or illegally. They are shown in Figure 2.11.

Any drug may cause harm if it is used improperly. As well as treating illness, some drugs produce physical and psychological side-effects. Some of these side-effects are very serious and can be life-threatening where the drug is misused.

All of the drugs shown in Figure 2.11 can be obtained illegally. Taken over prolonged periods, it is easy to become psychologically dependent upon them. People who try to stop taking them may suffer very unpleasant side-effects and withdrawal symptoms.

121

Figure 2.11: Commonly misused medicinal drugs		
Type of drug	**Example**	**Effects/dangers**
Barbiturates	Seconal	Normally used for severe sleeping problems or to stabilise epilepsy. Users can develop physical and mental dependence.
Tranquillisers/ Benzodiazepines	Valium	Used to counteract anxiety. If used over a long period users can come to depend on them rather than on non-drug coping methods.
Anabolic steroids	Stanozolol	Abused by some athletes and bodybuilders. While they can increase muscle size in ill or underweight people, they also stimulate aggression and can cause depression, jaundice and reproductive problems in men and women.
Amphetamines	Dexedrine	These drugs have very limited medical use. They are occasionally used to control hyperactivity in children and severe, chronic sleepiness in adults. They cause dependence and a range of physical and mental problems, including paranoia.
Opiates	Morphine	These drugs have a medical use as painkillers. Morphine may be abused because it gives the user a feeling of euphoria and mental well-being. It is very addictive. Overuse can cause nausea, breathing problems and vomiting.

The **Misuse of Drugs Act 1971** bans the non-medical use of certain prescription drugs, referred to as controlled drugs. The sale or possession of a controlled drug with intention to supply is a criminal offence.

Misuse of illegal drugs

Non-prescription illegal drugs are substances used to produce feelings of mental pleasure, stimulation and physical energy. These drugs have some short-term effects that users find pleasurable. However, their longer-term effects present major risks to users because of their damaging impact on physical health and on social, psychological and financial well-being.

Misuse of solvents

Solvents have many industrial and scientific applications. They are used in the production of cleaning fluids and in ink and paints. Solvents also are the main drugs that young people are most likely to experiment with after alcohol and tobacco.

Figure 2.12: Some common illegal drugs

Cannabis (dope, pot, hash, grass) is the most commonly used of the illegal drugs. It is a hard brown resinous material or herbal mixture. It causes users to feel more relaxed and talkative, reduces their ability to carry out complicated tasks and induces a sense of well-being with a heightened perception of music and colour.

Amphetamines (speed) are the most common illegal stimulant. They are usually found as a white or brown powder but can be in pill or capsule form. Amphetamines can be sniffed or injected and are addictive. They cause the user to experience disturbed sleep, loss of appetite, increased breathing and heart rate, a rise in blood pressure and sometimes feelings of acute anxiety and paranoia.

Magic mushrooms are hallucinogenic. They are a type of mushroom containing a substance similar to LSD. They grow wild in parts of the United Kingdom. It is not illegal to pick and eat them. The mushrooms contain the drug psilocybin, which has an hallucinogenic effect. They give the user varying experiences, from visions of joy and beauty to over-excitement after high doses. They may induce vomiting and severe stomach pains.

LSD (d-lysergic acid diethylamide) is another commonly used hallucinogen. It is a manufactured substance. Minute quantities of LSD are impregnated into small squares of blotting paper which are then dissolved on the tongue. These may distort vision and result in a feeling of being outside the body. 'Bad trips' can lead to depression, dizziness and panic attacks.

Ecstasy (methylenedioxymethamphetamine) is found as white, pink, or yellow tablets or as coloured capsules. Its effects can include a feeling of energy with heightened perception of colour and sound. It can also cause users to feel hot and thirsty and lead them to consume dangerously large quantities of fluids.

Cocaine is a powerful stimulant with properties similar to those of amphetamines. It is a white powder made from the leaves of the Andean coca shrub. Sometimes users inject it but more often it is inhaled. Users experience feelings of mental exhilaration and well-being, an indifference to pain and illusions of physical and mental strength. Cocaine is highly addictive and induces dependence. Severe anxiety and panic are two of its side-effects.

Most solvents and the solutions they form are liquids, but there are some solutions of gases or solids. Solvent-based products that are available and which are misused are:

- aerosol sprays (for example, hair sprays or pain-relieving spray)
- butane gas (used as cigarette lighter fuel)
- solvent-based glues
- dry-cleaning fluids
- paint and paint thinners
- correction fluids
- petrol.

The Intoxicating Substances Supply Act 1985 makes it an offence to supply substances which the supplier knows, or has reason to believe, will be used to achieve intoxication by a young person under the age of 18. The law, although mainly directed at shopkeepers, could be applied to anyone who sells or gives a young person a solvent-based product. Solvent misuse has a number of effects and dangers which are similar to those associated with alcohol.

- Butane gas, sprayed in the mouth, cools the throat tissues causing swelling and perhaps suffocation.
- Some solvents contain poisonous substances such as lead.
- Solvents induce a feeling of recklessness, making the user less able to deal with danger.
- Solvents are flammable. There is an increased fire risk if the user is smoking.
- Hallucinations may be caused.
- Disorientation may increase the risk from hazards in dangerous environments, for example, railway lines.
- Long-term use can cause damage to liver, kidneys, lungs, bone marrow and nervous system.

Tobacco

The smoking of tobacco, usually as cigarettes, is currently a major cause of ill health, disease and death in the western world. The use of tobacco is now less widespread and socially acceptable than it was twenty years ago. However, in 1996–7, just under 30 per cent of adults were still smokers and there were over 120,000 smoking-related deaths. Tobacco use is therefore a major cause of preventable disease and early death in the United Kingdom. The health problems associated with smoking include:

- coronary heart disease
- stroke
- high blood pressure
- bronchitis
- lung cancer
- other cancers, such as cancer of the larynx, kidney and bladder.

The harmful substances in tobacco and cigarette smoke affect the health of the person who is smoking and the health of non-smokers breathing in the smoke. These substances include **nicotine**, carbon monoxide and tar.

Nicotine is a powerful, fast-acting and addictive drug. When

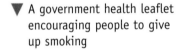

▼ A government health leaflet encouraging people to give up smoking

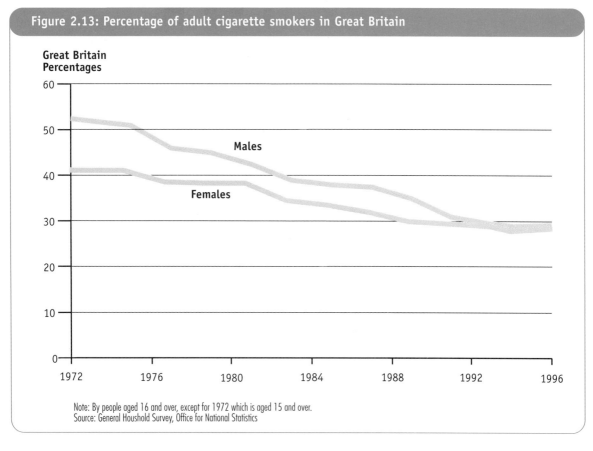

Figure 2.13: Percentage of adult cigarette smokers in Great Britain

Great Britain
Percentages

Males

Females

Note: By people aged 16 and over, except for 1972 which is aged 15 and over.
Source: General Houshold Survey, Office for National Statistics

smoked, it is absorbed into the bloodstream and its effects on the brain are felt seven to eight minutes later. The immediate effects of absorbing nicotine into the blood are:

- increase in heart rate and therefore an increase in blood pressure
- increase in hormone production
- constriction of the small blood vessels under the skin
- changes in blood composition with possibility of formation of blood clots in the vessels
- changes in appetite, either an increase or a decrease.

Carbon monoxide is a poisonous gas which is found in high concentrations in cigarette smoke. It combines readily with haemoglobin, the substance in the blood that carries oxygen. Because carbon monoxide combines more easily with haemoglobin than oxygen, the amount of oxygen carried to the lungs and tissues is reduced. A reduction in oxygen supply to the body affects the growth and repair of tissues, and the exchange of essential nutrients.

Carbon monoxide can also affect the activity of the heart. The changes in the blood that are associated with smoking may cause fat deposits to form on the walls of the arteries. This can lead to hardening of the arteries and to circulatory problems.

Cigarette tar contains many substances known to cause cancer. It damages the cilia, the small hairs lining the lungs that help to protect them from dirt and infection. As a result, smokers are more susceptible to throat and chest infections. About 70 per cent of the tar in a cigarette is deposited in the lungs when cigarette smoke is inhaled.

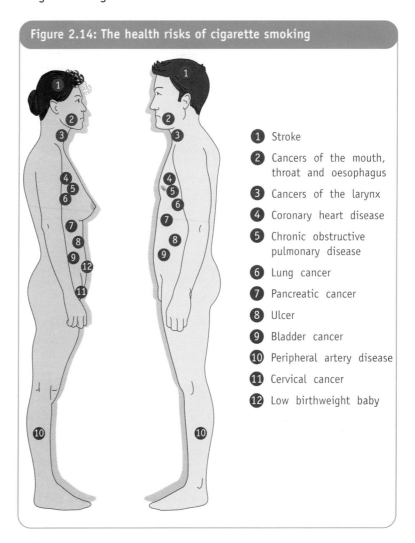

Figure 2.14: The health risks of cigarette smoking

1 Stroke
2 Cancers of the mouth, throat and oesophagus
3 Cancers of the larynx
4 Coronary heart disease
5 Chronic obstructive pulmonary disease
6 Lung cancer
7 Pancreatic cancer
8 Ulcer
9 Bladder cancer
10 Peripheral artery disease
11 Cervical cancer
12 Low birthweight baby

Smoking during pregnancy

When women smoke during pregnancy, the ability of the blood to carry oxygen to all parts of the body is reduced. This affects the flow of blood to the placenta which feeds the fetus. Mothers who smoke are at risk of suffering a miscarriage. Babies born to women who smoke can be premature and underweight and are more prone to upper respiratory tract infections. The risk of cot death to these babies is also increased.

Young people and smoking

Young people who take up smoking at a very early age run a
much greater risk of becoming addicted to the effects of
nicotine. They may also find that, they are beginning a lifelong
dependency on tobacco. In 1996, there were 1.7 million under-
age smokers in England. The younger a person starts to smoke,
the more cigarettes they will smoke and that increases the risk
of ill health and death. Once they start smoking, young people
immediately put themselves at risk of suffering minor illnesses,
such as coughing and shortness of breath. They are at greater
risk from serious diseases such as coronary heart disease, lung
cancer and chronic bronchitis in later life.

Figure 2.15: Percentage of children in England who regularly smoke

	1982	1986	1992	1996
Males				
Age 11	1	–	–	1
Age 12	2	2	2	2
Age 13	8	5	6	8
Age 14	18	6	14	13
Age 15	24	18	21	28
All males aged 11 to 15	11	7	9	11
Females				
Age 11	–	–	–	–
Age 12	1	2	2	4
Age 13	6	5	9	11
Age 14	14	16	15	24
Age 15	25	27	25	33
All females aged 11 to 15	11	12	10	15

Note: Regular means usually smoking at least one cigarette a week
Source: Smoking Among Secondary School Children Survey, Office for National Statistics

Passive smoking

Passive smoking means breathing in other people's cigarette smoke. This may be smoke from the burning end of the cigarette (sidestream smoke) or smoke inhaled and exhaled by the smoker (mainstream smoke). As this smoke is not being filtered, it is worse than smoking itself. Passive smoking can result in nose, throat, and eye irritation, headaches, dizziness and sickness, increased risk of coronary heart disease, chronic cough and wheezing in babies. Conditions such as asthma and other allergies are usually made worse.

Alcohol

Alcohol is a socially accepted drug which is widely used in the United Kingdom. Research shows that 98 per cent of the adult population use alcohol. There is a huge industry involved in the production and sale of alcoholic drinks.

Drinking alcohol in small quantities can be a pleasurable social experience. When consumed in large quantities, however, alcohol can have an adverse effect on personal health. Safe limits of alcohol consumption have been published by the Health Education Authority and are supported by health care professionals.

The recommended limits for women are two to three units a day, or less, and for men, between three and four units a day or less. One small glass of wine, half a pint of ordinary strength lager, beer or cider, or a 25 ml pub measure of spirit contain one unit of alcohol. If men and women follow this guide there should be no significant risks to their health. However, if women regularly drink three or more units and men drink four or more units a day, the risk to health is increased.

Studies have shown that people who regularly drink small amounts of alcohol tend to live longer than people who don't drink at all. This is because alcohol protects against the development of coronary heart disease. It also has an effect on the amount of cholesterol, or fat, carried in the bloodstream and therefore, makes it less likely that the clots which cause heart disease will form. Maximum health advantage can be achieved from drinking between one and two units of alcohol a day. There is no additional overall health benefit to be gained from drinking more than two units of alcohol a day.

The effects of alcohol on the body

Alcohol is rapidly absorbed into the bloodstream. The amount of alcohol that is concentrated in the body at any one time depends on:

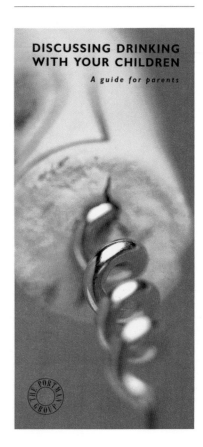

▼ The Portman Group encourages a sensible attitude to drinking

DISCUSSING DRINKING WITH YOUR CHILDREN

A guide for parents

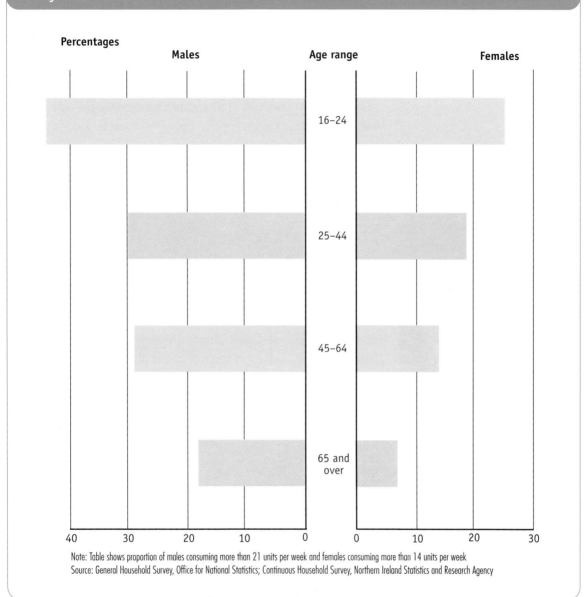

Figure 2.16: Proportion of adults in the United Kingdom consuming more than the recommended weekly levels of alcohol

Note: Table shows proportion of males consuming more than 21 units per week and females consuming more than 14 units per week
Source: General Household Survey, Office for National Statistics; Continuous Household Survey, Northern Ireland Statistics and Research Agency

- how much a person drinks
- whether the stomach is empty or full
- the height, weight, age and sex of the drinker.

Nearly all the alcohol that a person drinks has to be burnt up by the liver. The rest is disposed of either in sweat or urine. The body gets rid of one unit of alcohol in one hour. Smaller than average people, younger or older people and people who are not used to drinking are more easily affected by alcohol.

Alcohol is a **depressant**. It reduces certain brain functions and affects judgement, self-control and coordination. It is because of this that many fights, domestic violence, injuries and accidents result from excessive use of alcohol. It has been estimated that up to 40,000 deaths per year could be alcohol related. In 1996, 15 per cent of fatal road accidents involved driving with alcohol.

Drinking too much alcohol regularly increases the risk to health from:

- high blood pressure
- coronary heart disease
- liver damage and **cirrhosis** of the liver
- cancer of the mouth and throat
- psychological and emotional problems, including depression
- obesity.

▼ A balanced diet is vital to health

ENJOY HEALTHY EATING

THE BALANCE OF GOOD HEALTH

Diet

A good, balanced diet, that is, one containing adequate amounts of all the nutrients, is an important factor in protecting health and well-being. The type of diet and the amount of fruit and vegetables that people eat has an important influence on health. Unhealthy diets, those which tend to include too much salt, sugar and fatty foods and those lacking in fibre, are linked to cancers of the bowel, heart disease, stroke and tooth decay. Research suggests that a third of all cancers are the result of poor diet.

Stress

Stress is the general response of the body to any demand made upon it, whether it is physical or mental, pleasant or unpleasant. A stressful situation might be running for the bus, attending an interview, waiting for an important examination result, going to the dentist or to a doctor for a blood test. In such a situation a person might feel a variety of things all at once. For example, the stomach churns over, muscles are tensed, the heart beats faster, the skin sweats, the face flushes, and there are feelings of nausea.

Occasional stress is a normal part of human life. A certain amount is necessary and stimulating and most people are able to cope with it. However, stress becomes harmful when it is continuous, disrupts everyday life and relationships and becomes difficult to cope with. Whether a situation gives rise to harmful stress depends on the person's ability to cope with it, how prolonged the disturbance is, and the level of stress involved. In situations where stress persists for too long or is too intense, it may contribute to many disorders, including:

- anxiety and depression
- eczema
- asthma
- migraine
- poor sleep pattern
- angina (pain around the heart muscle)
- high blood pressure
- heart attack
- stomach ulcers
- accidents.

Lack of physical exercise

Research evidence suggests that physical inactivity can lead to ill health and disease. Physical inactivity is responsible for an increase in the risks of:

- coronary heart disease
- stroke
- obesity (excessively overweight, very fat)
- osteoporosis (brittle bones).

The Allied Dunbar National Fitness Survey (1995) identified several barriers that prevented people from taking more physical activity. These include insufficient time, dislike of sport and fear of injury. The survey found that an estimated 70 per cent or more of both men and women in all age groups took less than the acceptable level of activity required to keep them physically fit.

Health and hygiene

Personal hygiene

Good personal hygiene is a basic element of health and well-being. The main purpose of washing and cleaning regularly is to control the growth of bacteria, fungi and viruses that can cause illness and disease. The body provides the necessary conditions for the growth of bacteria and fungi. These are:

- moisture from sweat
- warmth from body heat
- food from the dead cells and waste products in sweat.

Washing and cleaning the body on a daily basis is essential to achieve good hygiene. The areas of the body that most need cleaning are those where sweat is excreted. These are under the arms, the groin area, the feet and the scalp and hair.

▼ Lack of physical activity can lead to obesity

Dental care and hygiene

Daily dental care is an important part of personal cleanliness. Brushing the teeth properly and using dental floss keeps the teeth clean and helps to prevent decay and gum disease.

Tooth decay begins with small holes, or **cavities**, which appear in the tooth enamel. The cavities are caused by bacteria on the tooth surface. Certain bacteria are naturally present in the mouth. Their job is to act on and break down the food we eat. In breaking down the food, the bacteria produce an acid. This acid attacks the enamel on the teeth, causing it to dissolve away in patches, forming cavities. The cavities reduce the distance between the outside of the tooth and the nerve endings. The acids produced by the bacteria irritate the nerve endings and cause toothache.

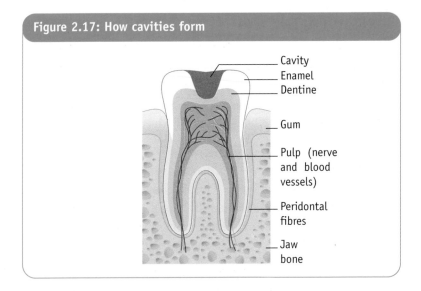

Figure 2.17: How cavities form

- Cavity
- Enamel
- Dentine
- Gum
- Pulp (nerve and blood vessels)
- Peridontal fibres
- Jaw bone

The best way to prevent tooth decay is to avoid eating sugar. The large amount of refined sugar in western diets causes a high level of tooth decay. Brushing with a fluoride toothpaste helps to increase the resistance of the enamel to bacterial acids. Regular visits to the dentist also help to ensure adequate dental care.

Skin care and hygiene

The skin forms a protective barrier for the body against bacteria and other chemicals. Glands in the skin release sweat containing waste products when the body becomes too hot. Harmful organisms may invade the body through areas where the skin has been broken. Others remain on the surface of the skin and dirt and debris accumulates in large quantities. A daily bath or shower keeps the body free from dirt and odour.

It also helps to prevent the skin infections that may develop if bacteria are allowed to grow and multiply on the skin.

Hair care and hygiene

Hair is protected from damage by a substance called sebum. This is the greasy substance that occurs naturally in everyone's hair. When we comb our hair the sebum is spread through it. Washing the hair removes the sebum. While hair must be washed and dressed regularly to remove dirt and the bacteria that use the sebum as food, a balance must be found between washing and combing the sebum through the hair.

Hygiene for children

Sandra Davis is a single mother of three children. She has just got a job and needs to arrange childcare for the time that she will be at work. You are one of three people who have answered her advert for a childminder for Dion, aged three, Sonia, aged six, and Jay, aged nine.

In the interview, Sandra explains the arrangements. The children would arrive at your house at about 8.30 a.m. Sandra would pick them up again after work at 4 p.m. Sandra's next questions is: 'What will you do to ensure that each of my children maintains good personal hygiene throughout the day?'

Write an answer explaining what you think the priorities are and indicate what you would do to set and maintain standards of good hygiene practice for each child.

Unsafe practices in the workplace

Under the Health And Safety At Work Act 1974, all employers have a responsibility to ensure, as far as is reasonably practicable, the health, safety and welfare of all workers and those affected by their work, and everyone who uses their setting, including:

- employees
- children in their care
- parents
- students and other helpers
- visitors
- the public, if they are affected.

HSC
Health & Safety
Commission

Health and Safety
at Work etc Act

Advice to
employers

▲ A leaflet produced by the
Health and Safety Executive

The Act is directly enforced by the Health and Safety Executive or, where appropriate, it may be delegated to local authority health and safety officers. They will ensure that the workplace has an effective system for the provision of health and safety, the maintenance and use of the premises and equipment.

Employers, providers of services and self-employed people should take all reasonable steps to ensure that:

- no one is exposed to risks as a result of their work
- any premises are kept safe to prevent risks to all users
- the equipment is not dangerous and the manufacturer's instructions for use are followed
- everyone is instructed and informed in all matters of health and safety
- all accidents, falls, cuts and bruises are recorded in the appropriate accident and incident report book
- fire precautions are observed.

Similarly, all employees and care workers have a duty to take reasonable care of themselves and any others who might be affected by their work. They must ensure that no unsafe practices are followed in the workplace. They should cooperate with their employers and must not interfere with, or misuse equipment in a way which might be dangerous to themselves, other care workers or service users.

Public hygiene

The term **public health** refers to all the actions taken to maintain and improve the general health of a community. The local authority environmental health department ensures that high standards of hygiene are maintained in places such as restaurants, pubs and hairdressing salons.

Food preparation

Cleanliness of the kitchen and kitchen equipment is vital for safe food preparation. Any area where food is prepared should be cleaned at regular intervals to reduce the amount of dirt brought in. Refrigerators, ovens, floors and other equipment used in direct handling of food must receive thorough and regular cleaning.

Strict guidelines for food preparation and storage are enforced by local authority environmental health officers. In an organisation where food is prepared, general cleanliness of the entire building and the adequate provision of washing and food storage facilities, are important to prevent food-borne illnesses and diseases. To reduce risk and to minimise contamination of food, the following measures should be observed.

- Wash hands before and after the preparation of food.
- Follow the storage guidelines on food packages.
- Quickly cool and refrigerate any left-over food.
- Allow food removed from a refrigerator to thaw out to room temperature.
- Store meats in the bottom of the refrigerator.
- Cover or tie back hair.
- Keep cuts and wounds covered.
- Avoid food preparation if you are suffering from any type of infection or infectious disease.
- Clean surfaces on which food is prepared after use.
- Use a separate preparation board for poultry products.

Hygiene in care settings

Health workers who care directly for patients must take precautions and observe recommended basic hygiene practice to counter the risk of infection. Nurses, doctors and other health workers in accident and emergency departments and those involved in surgical, gynaecological and obstetrics procedures must take all precautions to avoid the risk of infection because they are likely to come into contact with body fluids and open wounds.

In care settings health workers can protect themselves and reduce the risk of catching and transmitting infections to their clients by:

- washing their hands after using the toilet or helping another person to do so, when changing beds or touching used bed linen, and before eating or preparing a meal for themselves or others
- wearing disposable gloves, masks, aprons and other protective clothing when dealing with body fluids and wounds
- putting used linen and clothes in the correct bags to protect laundry workers
- using the correct bags and bins to dispose of waste; dressings and other clinical waste should always be put in bags that will be incinerated
- reporting broken equipment, spills and pest infestations immediately
- always following hygiene rules when storing and preparing food, reporting outbreaks of illness and infection immediately.

▼ Disposable gloves and aprons help to counter the risk of infection

Health and safety in the home

▶ Safety poster produced by the Royal Society for the Prevention of Accidents

Safety in the home is of particular importance for all the occupants and visitors to the home but is especially so for infants and young children, the elderly and people with special needs. This is because their well-being is directly affected by a safe environment. You will remember that accidents are the most common cause of death in people under 30 and an important cause of injury and disability, particularly in young children aged three to nine and in the elderly aged over 65. Any accident, even if it results in minor injuries, may have an immediate effect on a child's health. Serious accidents and injuries may result in increased anxiety and stress for the child and his or her family. It is important to make the home safe and prevent accidents by:

- identifying sources of potential danger and correcting them
- ensuring that small and sharp objects that babies and infants can swallow are not left lying around
- locking away all medicines and poisonous substances such as bleach and other cleaning agents that can be accidentally swallowed
- ensuring that babies and infants are not left unsupervised
- ensuring that plastic bags which present a danger of suffocation to children are kept out of their reach
- storing all inflammable items such as matches, lighters, petrol and methylated spirits away out of reach of children
- installing safety gates to prevent infants from falling downstairs
- using non-slip mats in the bath to prevent slipping
- using safety pads on unused electric sockets
- using fireguards on electric and open fires
- ensuring that there are no loose carpets on which an elderly person might trip.

Sexual behaviour

All of us have sexual needs which need to find expression in some way. Developing a sexual relationship with another person is one way of expressing intimate feelings. Choosing to be sexually active involves taking some personal risks. For example, in a heterosexual relationship there is the risk of unwanted pregnancy. The main risk to health that sexual activity presents is from sexually transmitted diseases.

Figure 2.18: New cases of sexually transmitted diseases reported in England and Wales

	1995	1996	1997	1998
Males				
Genital warts	26,178	26,757	30,075	30,906
Non-specific genital infection	66,963	70,721	77,599	n/a
Chlamydia	12,735	13,772	16,105	19,043
Herpes simplex	5,886	5,678	5,561	6,085
Gonorrhoea	6,613	7,784	8,367	8,362
Infectious syphilis	102	84	97	83
Antigen positive hepatitis B	519	446	608	578
Females				
Genital warts	24,988	27,272	28,341	29,070
Non-specific genital infection	37,584	40,594	46,609	n/a
Chlamydia	16,478	18,320	22,527	25,136
Herpes simplex	9,113	9,393	9,432	9,620
Gonorrhoea	3,325	3,926	3,949	4,038
Infectious syphilis	30	32	49	49
Antigen positive hepatitis B	177	194	185	306

Source: Public Health Laboratory Service, Communicable Disease Surveillance Centre

There are at least thirty different types of sexually transmitted disease. They affect about one million men and women in the United Kingdom every year. Research shows that young people between the ages of 15 and 30 are most likely to be affected. The most common is chlamydia. It can cause serious problems such as **pelvic inflammatory disease (PID)** and inflammation of the fallopian tubes if it is not treated.

Figure 2.19: Sexually transmitted diseases

Disease	Symptoms	Cause	Treatment
Thrush (candida albicans)	A thick, white discharge from the vagina, itching, swelling, soreness and pain around the vulva on urination.	Candida.	Anti-fungal creams, pessaries or tablets inserted into the vagina.
Genital warts	Small hard spots on the lips or inside of the vagina or around the anus. In men they may appear on the scrotum.	Virus transmitted through intimate physical contact.	Ointments can be applied to infected areas or the warts may be removed by freezing, burning or surgery.
Genital herpes	A burning sensation and pain in the infected area. Small red bumps develop into blisters or painful open sores on the penis or in the vagina and around the genitals.	Herpes simplex virus transmitted through intimate contact.	Drug treatment, either an ointment or tablets.
Gonorrhoea	Pain or burning sensation when urinating. Also discharge from vagina or penis. Women may also have pain in the lower abdomen.	A bacteria transmitted by intimate physical contact that grows rapidly in moist warm areas such as the cervix.	A course of antibiotic tablets, with a follow-up to check infection is cleared.
Hepatitis B	Flu-like symptoms two to three months after infection. Jaundice later appears with yellow discoloration of the skin and eyes.	A virus in the blood or other body fluids transmitted by intimate physical contact.	Bed rest, plenty of fluids. Vaccinations are recommended.
Pubic lice	Itching in the pubic area. Lice eggs on the base of pubic hairs.	Lice mites laying eggs and being transferred during close physical contact.	Medicated lotions and shampoos.
Syphilis	A painless sore on the penis, vulva, vagina, cervix, tongue or fingertips two to six weeks after contact with the infection.	Bacteria transmitted during intimate physical contact.	A course of penicillin treatment.
Chlamydia	A slight increase in vaginal discharge caused by the inflammation of the cervix (the neck of the uterus). A need to pass urine more often, pain on passing urine, lower abdominal pain, pain during sexual intercourse, irregular bleeding between periods, painful swelling and irritation in the eyes (if they are infected).	Bacteria transmitted through intimate physical contact. Infection can also be transferred on fingers from the genitals to the eye and from a mother to her baby at birth.	A course of antibiotic tablets, with a follow-up to check infection is cleared.

Figure 2.19 summarises some of the different types of sexually transmitted diseases, their causes, symptoms, and treatment.

Sexually transmitted diseases can affect both men and women, whether they are heterosexual or homosexual. The risk of contracting an infection is not confined only to people with many sexual partners, although they do run a greater risk. A person can become infected with a sexually transmitted disease after a single act of unprotected sex with another infected person.

ACTIVITY

Taking risks with sex

Why do you think that some teenagers take risks with sex? Discuss this in a small group.

Compare your ideas with those of other groups in the class. Make a list of the most common reasons discussed in the various groups.

If you had to advise a group of teenagers about the risks associated with sexual activity, what are the five things you would consider most important and why?

HIV and AIDS

The newest and most challenging sexually transmitted disease is the human immunodeficiency virus (HIV). This is the virus which causes acquired immune deficiency syndrome (AIDS). The virus, a simple living organism, gets into the bloodstream and attacks and destroys the body's natural defence mechanisms. HIV can be transmitted through three different routes.

- **Unprotected sex** involving penetration (anal or vaginal) and the release of infected semen or vaginal secretions into the body. People who do not use condoms or spermicides during sex run a higher risk of catching the virus this way.
- **Infected blood** can enter the body through a cut or other wound. People who inject drugs and use infected needles and syringes run a high risk of catching the virus through this route.
- **During pregnancy**. Before, during or after birth, an infected mother can pass on the virus to her baby through breast milk or blood.

139

Figure 2.20: Incidence of AIDS and HIV in the United Kingdom

Probable HIV exposure category	Male		Female		Deaths in
	AIDS	HIV	AIDS	HIV	AIDS cases
Sex between men	10,736	19,582			8,181
Sex between men and women					1,535
Exposure to high risk partners	65	150	215	647	
Exposure abroad	1,220	2,700	942	2,729	
Exposure in the UK	110	255	129	401	
Others/no further information	32	187	25	218	
Injecting drug use (IDU)	726	2,273	298	1,030	731
IDU and sex between men	286	523			
Blood factor (such as haemophilia)	638	1,337	6	11	585
Blood/tissue transfer (blood transfusions)	57	109	84	119	106
Mother to infant	148	269	156	272	137
Other/undetermined	136	724	19	183	121
All categories	14,154	28,109	1,874	5,610	11,396

Note: Figures to the end of December 1998
Source: Public Health Laboratory Service

Many people who have HIV (who are HIV positive) have no symptoms of illness and live healthy lives for many years. Some have never developed AIDS and continue to be healthy. Others may present symptoms and be unwell due to the virus. By the end of 1998, there had been 11,396 AIDS-related deaths in the United Kingdom and, in total, nearly 50,000 people were reported to have been infected by the HIV virus.

The following measures can be taken to reduce the risk of contracting HIV in the care workplace.

- Practice good basic hygiene, regularly washing hands.
- Cover all existing wounds or skin lesions with waterproof dressings when in contact with body fluids.
- Avoid contamination of clothing by using protective garments, such as aprons.
- Follow approved procedures for sterilisation and disinfection of instruments and equipment.
- Follow correct procedures for the safe disposal of contaminated waste.
- Avoid using sharp instruments whenever possible.
- Follow safe procedures for handling and disposal of needles.
- Clear up all spills of blood and other body fluids promptly and disinfect surfaces thoroughly.

Build your learning

Summary points

- Misuse of drugs, whether they are legally prescribed or illegal, smoking and drinking excessive amounts of alcohol can put people's health at risk.

- People's health is also at risk if they eat an unbalanced diet, fail to take physical exercise, or if they engage in unsafe sexual behaviours.

- Smoking, whether active or passive, carries serious risks to health, including bronchitis, cancer, high blood pressure, heart disease, and stroke.

Key words and phrases

You should know the meaning of the words and phrases listed below as they relate to factors which can present an increased risk to an individual's health and well-being.

- Depressant
- Misuse of Drugs Act 1971
- Side-effects
- Health and Safety At Work Act 1974
- Nicotine

- Sebum
- Haemoglobin
- Public health
- Passive smoking
- Pelvic inflammatory disease

- Uterus
- Obesity
- Osteoporosis
- Cavities
- Cirrhosis
- Cervix

Student questions

1 What is the purpose of the Misuse of Drugs Act 1971?

2 What are the side-effects of amphetamines?

3 Make a list of the different solvent-based products that can be misused.

4 Make a list of the health problems associated with smoking.

5 Explain what you understand by safe limits of alcohol for adults.

6 What are the symptoms and complications of chlamydia?

ASSESSMENT WORK

Identifying factors affecting individual health

An individual's health and well-being are influenced by a variety of physical, social and economic factors. Some of these, such as whether a person takes exercise, are under the control of the individual whilst others, such as environmental pollution, are less controllable. This activity gives you an opportunity to undertake some research to find out about factors that influence the health and well-being of one individual.

The work that you do here will become a part of your end of unit assignment.

	Assessment criteria	Which tasks do I need to do?
Pass	Understand the factors that affect the health and well-being of your chosen person by considering physical factors and at least one social and emotional factor.	**1a**
Pass	Explain clearly factors which cause potential risks to the health and well-being of your chosen person.	**1b**

Key skills

C2.1a, C2.2, C2.3, IT2.2, IT2.3

It may be possible to claim these key skills for this coursework depending on how you have completed the tasks and presented your work. Your teacher will need to check your evidence against the key skills specification.

What to do

1a Conduct an interview with your volunteer about his or her background, lifestyle and health behaviour. You need to cover as many of the factors that affect health that we discussed earlier (see pages 103–18) as you can. Explain how these factors have an effect on the health and well-being of your chosen person.

1b Are there any features of your volunteer's background, life circumstances or behaviour that could be considered a risk to his or her health or well-being? (See pages 120–31 for ideas.) Again, explain how these factors may have a negative effect on the health and well-being of your chosen person.

You should base this assessment work on an individual who is willing to volunteer information about him or herself and who is able to fully understand what the activity involves. You may also want to complete the assessment preparation activity about taking and interpreting health measures (see page 149) when you meet with your volunteer to obtain information.

If you carry out these activities now you will have partly completed the work needed for your end of unit assignment.

Indicators of physical good health

So far we've looked at those factors that influence health and those that put health at risk. We've talked about these in some detail but haven't said how good physical health can be measured. How are health care workers able to tell if an individual is healthy or not? There are, in fact, many different ways of measuring health. In this section we look at a number of techniques for measuring physical health.

Measuring good health

When measuring an individual's health status a health care worker will generally take some physical and physiological measurements and then compare the individual's 'score' against a standard scale. We now look at some of the key indicators of good health that are often measured and compared.

Child growth rates

Centile charts are used to assess the growth rates of babies and young children. A centile chart is a standard scale that gives an indication of the average growth rates of boys and girls in the British population. Measuring a child's weight and height and checking it against a centile chart is one way of seeing if he or she is in good health. The regular assessment of stature is the most sensitive indicator of a child's well-being.

It is important to bear in mind that these charts are only based, for practical purposes, on the indigenous white British population and, unfortunately, do not include centiles for other ethnic minority communities. As a general rule of thumb, Asian babies and children are smaller and lighter, and African Caribbean babies and children are taller and heavier than white British babies.

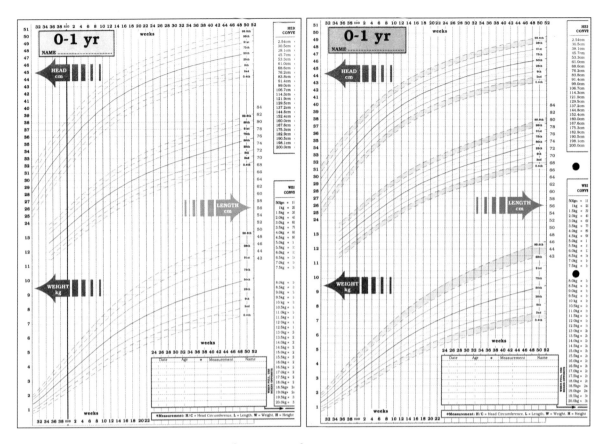

▲ Centile charts used for assessing the growth rates of children

Body mass index

In adults, the relationship between height and weight can be an indicator of good or ill health. A person's weight should be in proportion to his or her height (see Figure 2.21). A person is considered obese when his or her weight is more than 20 per cent above the average weight for people of the same height and similar personal and cultural characteristics. Health professionals use the **body mass index** (BMI) to assess whether a person is overweight. You can use the following formula to work out your BMI.

$$BMI = \frac{body\ weight\ (kg)}{(height)^2\ (m^2)}$$

Peak flow

A person's respiratory (breathing) health can be measured by using a peak flow meter. This measures the maximum rate at which air is expelled from the lungs when a person breathes out as hard as he or she can. The peak flow meter is one example of a **pulmonary function test**. These are used to monitor several aspects of respiratory function.

Figure 2.21: Are you the right weight for your height?

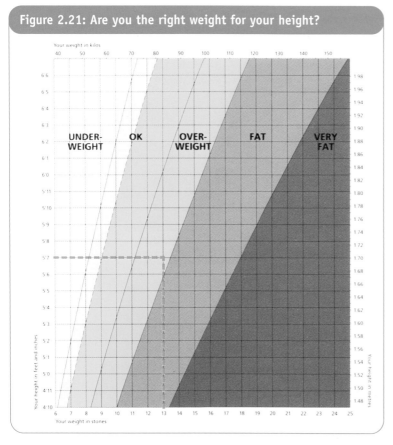

The peak flow meter can be used to diagnose whether a person has a problem with the use of his or her lungs, because there is a standard scale of expected scores against which the results can be compared. People with chronic (long-term) asthma usually record a measurement that is lower than 350.

◀ Using a peak flow meter

Pulse rate

The pulse rate is often used to determine a person's general health or physical fitness. The pulse rate indicates how fast the heart is beating. For adults, the rate, on average, is usually between 70 and 80 beats per minute when a person is at rest. The pulse can be taken recorded in any artery (see Figure 2.22). The radial artery at the wrist and the carotid artery at the neck are the commonly used pulse points. The pulse rate increases when a person exercises, when he or she is emotionally disturbed and when he or she has forms of heart and respiratory disease.

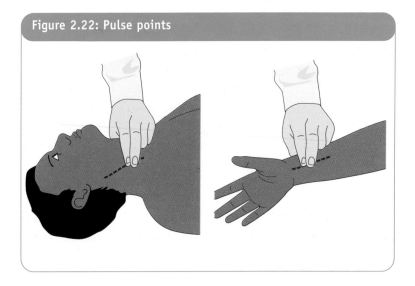

Figure 2.22: Pulse points

Blood pressure

Blood pressure is the force or pressure which the blood exerts on the walls of the artery in which it is contained. The pressure that blood continuously puts on the arteries is partly dependent on their elasticity and is called the diastolic pressure. The increase in pressure occurring when blood is forced out of the heart as it beats is called the systolic pressure. Together the diastolic and systolic pressure give a measure known as the blood pressure.

This measure is obtained by using an instrument called a sphygmomanometer ('sphyg' for short). This consists of a rubber bag which is placed around the arm. The interior of the bag is connected by a rubber tube to a mercury pressure gauge. This is gently inflated. When the pressure in the bag equals the pressure in the artery, the artery is gently compressed and the blood flow through it is temporarily arrested, causing the pulse at the wrist to disappear. A stethoscope is attached to the ear of the person taking the blood pressure, and placed over the brachial artery at the bend of the elbow. Each beat of the heart increases the pressure. The height to which the mercury has been forced at this moment, is the systolic blood pressure. The rubber tube is then gently deflated, during which time the mercury column falls and the heart beat gradually disappears. The last beat is the diastolic pressure. This is measured in millimetres. The blood pressure varies with the age of the individual. On average it measures 120/80 mm Hg (millimetres of mercury) in the young adult.

Recommended health behaviour

Certain behaviour patterns can be monitored and recorded to provide a health measure. For example, an individual's dietary intake, amount of exercise taken, and use of alcohol and tobacco can be compared against tables and scales of recommended intake, to assess the extent to which he or she is healthy. When assessing an individual's health, it is necessary to take the person's age, gender, sex, social class and ability/disability into consideration. As no two people are ever exactly alike, these measures should only be used as a guide to health status.

 Build your learning

Summary points

- Physical measures such as height, weight and the pulse rate can be used to determine the extent to which a person is physically healthy.

- The relationship between a person's height and weight is known as the body mass index. This can be used as an indicator of health.

- Pulmonary function tests, such as peak flow, are used to monitor the health of the respiratory system.

- The pulse rate measures the performance of the heart. It can be taken at any artery but is usually measured at the wrist and the carotid artery in the neck.

- Blood pressure is another measure indicating the health of the heart. It can be measured by using a sphygmomanometer.

Key words and phrases

You should know the meaning of the words and phrases listed below as they relate to some of the indicators and physical measures of good health. If you are not sure about any of them, go back through the last five pages to check or refresh your understanding.

- Pulmonary function test
- Centile charts
- Body mass index

- Systolic pressure
- Sphygmomanometer
- Diastolic pressure
- Blood pressure

- Radial artery
- Carotid artery
- Brachial artery

 Student questions

1 What does a centile chart measure tell you about a child's health?

2 How does a peak flow meter give an indication of a person's health?

3 What is the name of the artery where you would typically place the stethoscope when recording a person's blood pressure?

4 What does a person's pulse rate tell you about his or her health?

5 Name two ways of measuring health other than those referred to in questions 1 to 4.

ASSESSMENT WORK

Taking health measurements

This activity gives you an opportunity to demonstrate that you understand how to carry out some basic measures of physical health. Ideally you should use the same volunteer as you did in the previous assessment work activity on page 142. The work that you do here will become a part of your end of unit assignment.

UNIT TWO
ASSESSMENT WORK

	Assessment criteria	Which tasks do I need to do?
Pass	Correctly use and interpret the measures you have chosen.	2a 2b
Merit	Analyse how your chosen person's measures of health could be affected by a range of risks and factors.	2c

What to do

2a Carry out and record the following measures of physical health on your volunteer:

- height and weight
- pulse rate
- body mass index
- alcohol intake
- smoking habits.

2b What do the results tell you about your volunteer's physical health?

2c Identify the factors that are most influential in determining the results in each of these areas, for example, the amount and type of food eaten and exercise taken have a strong influence on weight.

You should base your work on an individual who is willing to volunteer information about him or herself and who is able to fully understand what the activity involves.

Key skills

N2.1, N2.2, N2.3, C2.2, C2.3

It may be possible to claim these key skills for this coursework depending on how you have completed the tasks and presented your work. Your teacher will need to check your evidence against the key skills specification.

take
that
first
step...

positive steps for feeling good

▲ This foot-shaped health promotion leaflet is designed to appeal to young people

Health promotion

Health promotion is a growing area of health care work. It is one way of providing information to individuals, groups, communities and the wider population, in order to raise their health status and improve their health and well-being.

Most of the large-scale health promotion work is carried out by government health promotion agencies. They use different media to put **health messages** across. You have probably seen evidence of many different health promotion campaigns in newspapers and magazines, on television or in booklets and posters. You may have come across them at your local leisure centre, sports ground, health centre, library, shopping centre, health food shop, school, college, home for the elderly, nursery, or youth club. You may have felt that some of these campaigns were aimed at people of your age-group or background.

Providing health information to others

Careful planning and preparation are essential for successful health promotion. Once a health promotion topic has been identified, the promotion team needs to:

- identify the key aims (what it wants to do) and objectives (what it wants to achieve) of the campaign
- decide the best way of putting the health message across
- identify the resources needed to deliver the health message
- decide how the effectiveness of the campaign will be evaluated (judged).

Choosing a presentation format

The health promotion campaign will be more effective if it is well prepared. The best method of getting the key health messages of the campaign across needs to be identified. Health promotion workers have used a variety of methods including:

- poster campaigns
- television and radio campaigns
- talks and lectures
- seminars
- workshops
- information films and videos
- information packs
- booklets and leaflets
- games and role plays
- promotional displays.

The health promotion team needs to choose the delivery method that will be most effective in reaching its particular target group.

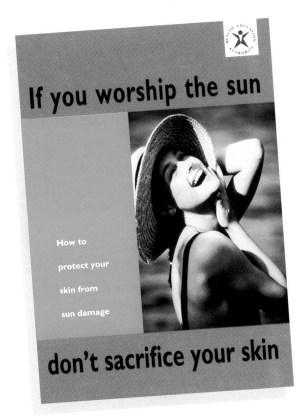

If you worship the sun

How to protect your skin from sun damage

don't sacrifice your skin

◀ Recent publicity campaigns have highlighted the potential danger of sunbathing

ACTIVITY

Effective health campaigns

Advertisements and promotional campaigns try to put across a distinctive message. Some do this in subtle ways, others do it in very strong, obvious ways. They try to persuade the person who is reading or watching the message to either do something or to think about something.

1 Make a list of the features you believe are important in making persuasive communications like adverts and health campaigns effective.

2 What is your favourite advertisement/health campaign? Identify the features you like and which make it memorable.

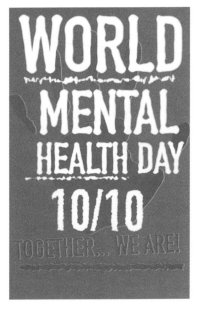

WORLD MENTAL HEALTH DAY 10/10 TOGETHER... WE ARE!

▲ A targeted health promotion flyer

Targeting health promotion advice and information

Health promotion campaigns tend to target specific groups in the population. The groups in the community that need specific advice on health topics are known as **target groups**. The health promotion message and the methods used to put it across, must appeal to the groups at whom it is targeted. In the past these have included:

- teenagers
- young people
- pregnant women
- smokers
- people who are obese
- people who have an alcohol problem
- the homeless
- travellers
- pre-retirement groups.

When planning a health promotion campaign for a specific group, the reasons for the campaign must be clearly identified from the outset. Reasons could be:

- to provide advice and support
- to supply information
- to help people to change or modify health-related behaviour.

There are many areas of health promotion which may be suitable to a specific group's needs. These might include:

- how to lose weight safely and quickly
- information about how to use the local health services
- how to lead an active life after disability
- the importance of cutting down on salt, or increasing fibre intake
- ways of keeping warm in winter
- preparation for retirement
- the benefits of exercise
- maintaining personal hygiene
- preventing dental problems
- getting the best out of sport and leisure facilities
- how to maintain desired weight in pregnancy.

Health advice for children

Choose any one of the following topics around which to develop a health message targeted at children:

- dental health

- balanced diet

- smoking

- exercise

- personal safety.

Identify a message that would promote good health and well-being in a group of children aged seven to nine years.

What methods could be used to get this message across to children of this age?

Assessing the impact of health promotion advice

Health promotion workers are usually concerned to assess the effectiveness of their campaigns. There are various ways of assessing how well health promotion advice has been received and understood. The aim is to gain feedback from the target audience on the effectiveness of the presentation. By acting on the feedback received, health promoters will be able to improve subsequent campaigns.

The impact of, say, a health promotion session can be assessed by verbal methods, such as asking questions at the end of the presentation to check understanding. These can be designed to find out the target group's views on the topic and the presentation. Alternatively, session participants can be asked to complete an evaluation questionnaire such as the one in Figure 2.23.

Figure 2.23: Health evaluation questionnaire

Please can you complete the following questionnaire to help in the assessment of the impact of this session and the design of further sessions.

Tick the appropriate box.

Evaluation of a health promotion session on:

1 I found the session: very useful ☐
                                        useful   ☐
                                        not useful   ☐

2 The most valuable part was:

3 The least valuable part was:

4 The session was: too long   ☐
                                        too short   ☐
                                        just right   ☐

5 The session added to my existing knowledge: yes ☐
                                                  no   ☐

6 The session will affect my behaviour: yes ☐
                                           no   ☐

7 I will act on the advice: yes ☐
                                       no   ☐

8 If you had to change any part of the session which would you change, how and why?

9 Please add any comments.

Thank you for completing this evaluation form.

Build your learning

Summary points

- Health promotion involves various ways of giving information to individuals, groups and communities on health and well-being topics.

- The messages that are contained in health promotion information usually try to encourage healthy behaviour and often try to get people to change their behaviour.

- Health promotion is carried out by specialist agencies and a wide range of health care workers.

- Health promotion is targeted at various groups and individuals who have a need for particular types of health information.

- Target groups might include teenagers, people who smoke, people who are obese and pregnant women.

Key words and phrases

You should know the meaning of the words and phrases listed below as they relate to health promotion. If you are not sure about any of them, go back through the last five pages to check or refresh your understanding.

- **Health messages**
- **Target groups**
- **Evaluation**
- **Presentation methods**
- **Health improvement targets**

Student questions

1 What is the general aim of health promotion campaigns?

2 Name four different methods used to promote health messages to the general public.

3 What do you feel would be the most effective method of giving anti-smoking advice and information to children?

4 What are health promoters trying to do when they evaluate their campaign?

5 Name two methods of evaluating a health promotion campaign.

ASSESSMENT WORK

Developing a health improvement plan

This activity gives you an opportunity to develop health improvement targets for an individual. You will need to produce a three-month plan that uses health promotion materials to support the achievement of the targets you set.

If you have completed assessment work activities 1 and 2 (see pages 142 and 149) you will be able to base your work for this activity on information you have already collected. The work that you do here will become a part of your end of unit assignment. You can gain a pass, merit or distinction grade by completing the tasks indicated.

	Assessment criteria	Which tasks do I need to do?
Pass	Communicate your plan in a form appropriate to your chosen person and explain how the targets can be met.	3a
Pass	Clearly explain why the health promotion materials were selected.	3b
Merit	Prioritise short and long-term targets with timescales, giving reasons for the targets chosen.	3c
Merit	Analyse the ways in which the chosen health promotion materials could support the plan.	3d
Distinction	Consider the physical, social and emotional effects on your chosen person of achieving the targets in the plan.	3e
Distinction	Anticipate potential difficulties in achieving the plan and propose realistic ways that they may be overcome.	3e

If you carry out the following activities now you will have completed part of the work needed for your end of unit assignment.

What to do

(3a) Produce a health improvement plan for your volunteer which:

- identifies the general areas in which the person's health could be improved
- suggests some overall health improvement targets for the person
- explains the general ways in which these targets could be met.

(3b) Select some health promotion materials which you feel could help your volunteer in his or her attempt to meet the overall health improvement targets you've identified. Explain your reasons for choosing these particular health promotion materials.

(3c) Break down your overall health improvement targets into smaller short-term and long-term targets for your volunteer to achieve. Put the targets in the order in which you would want them to be achieved (suggest dates) and briefly explain your reasons for choosing these targets.

(3d) Explain the different ways in which the health promotion materials that you've chosen could be used to help your volunteer achieve the short and long-term health improvement targets that you've identified.

(3e) Achieving the targets that you set in your health improvement plan will be challenging but, hopefully, beneficial to your volunteer:

- identify reasons why your volunteer may find achieving the targets difficult
- suggest some realistic ways in which these difficulties could be overcome
- describe the positive effects that achieving the health improvement targets would have on your on your chosen volunteer's health and well-being.

Self-assessment of evidence

What to do

To complete this unit you need to produce a plan for promoting health and well-being for at least one person. The plan must include:

- information about the risks to health, identifying those over which the individual may have control
- at least two measures of health
- timescales and targets for improvement
- supporting health promotion materials.

If you have completed the assessment work activities throughout the chapter (see pages 142, 149 and 156) you should have produced enough work for your report. You should organise the work that you've completed into an assignment. Ideally, your report should have:

- a cover and contents list
- an introduction explaining what the assignment is about
- a section on the factors affecting your chosen individual's health and well-being
- a section outlining a number of measures of physical health
- a section containing a health improvement plan for your chosen individual.

What can you achieve?

By checking through the work that you've done you can assess your evidence before your teacher or lecturer marks and grades it. This will help you to work out what you may be able to achieve for the overall end of unit assignment.

Page	Activity	Grade	Have I completed this? (Tick)
142	1a,1 b	Pass	☐
149	2a, 2b	Pass	☐
149	2c	Merit	☐
156	3a, 3b	Pass	☐
156	3c, 3d	Merit	☐
156	3e	Distinction	☐

You must complete all of the 'pass' grade activities to finish the unit. If you want to try and get a merit you must complete all of the pass grade activities and all of the merit grade activities. For a distinction you must complete every activity and produce a high standard of work. When you hand in your work your teacher or lecturer will mark it and decide whether you have met the assessment criteria and reached the required standard.

Understanding personal development 3

This unit will help you to develop your knowledge and understanding of human growth and personal development across the life span. You will learn about:

- human growth and personal development during the five main life stages

- social and economic factors influencing human growth and development

- development of the self-concept

- major life changes, their influence on personal development and the ways that people deal with them

- the types of support that promote development.

Health and social care workers are employed to work with people of all ages and backgrounds.

Some care workers specialise in working with a particular age group, such as children or older people. Other care workers specialise in a particular type of work, such as nursing, occupational therapy or physiotherapy. Whatever their speciality, all care workers should have an understanding of human growth and development.

The material covers Unit 3, Understanding Personal Development, of the GNVQ Intermediate full award and the GNVQ Intermediate Part One award.

Introduction to growth and development

In order to understand human growth and development you will need to understand the meaning of some key words and ideas that are commonly used by care workers.

People are said to go through a number of life stages during their life span. A life stage is a defined period of growth and development. The five main life stages in which major physical growth and personal development occur are:

- infancy (0–3 years)
- early childhood (3–8 years)
- puberty and adolescence
- adulthood
- old age (over 75 years).

These stages cover the whole of the human life span. This is the period between a person's birth and his or her death. Figure 3.1 shows that whilst people are living to an increasingly old age, women have a longer life span than men. Male children born in the period 1990–1992 have an expected life span of 73.4 years compared to 79 years for women born during the same period.

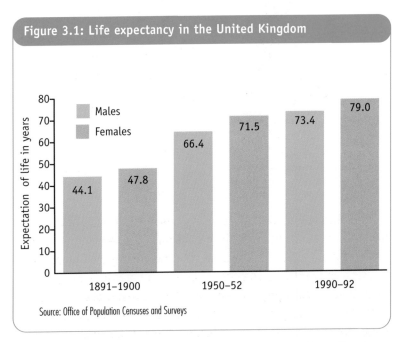

Figure 3.1: Life expectancy in the United Kingdom

Source: Office of Population Censuses and Surveys

There is an important difference between growth and development. Growth refers to the increase in physical size, or mass, that occurs as a person gradually moves from infancy through childhood into adulthood. Generally, people grow bigger in various ways. Development is different to growth. It refers to the way a person acquires new skills and capabilities. These become more sophisticated and complex as the person progresses towards adulthood.

Influences on human growth and development

What makes human beings grow and develop? There is a simple way of describing the major influences on human growth and development. People are said to grow and develop through the combined effects of nature and nurture.

Nature refers to biological, genetic influences on growth and development. We all inherit certain characteristics, abilities and predispositions from our parents. There is very little that we can do to change the physical features and growth potential that we inherit. If both of our biological parents are over six feet tall, have big feet and are fast runners, we are highly likely to also grow to that height, have large feet and be able to run fast because we will inherit these physical characteristics and abilities.

◀ Natural physical attributes play a very important role in some activities

The physical characteristics and growth potential that we have are given to us in the chromosomes that we inherit from our parents. This is nature at work. The timing of a person's physical growth, and the sequence in which things happen, including specific physical changes like starting menstruation and the beginning of the menopause, are also biologically controlled by the hormones that we have in our bodies.

Physical growth and change cannot, however, be fully explained by nature. Nurture also plays a role in our physical growth. This term refers to the powerful effect of environmental influences on our physical growth and personal development. For example, whilst the human growth process is strongly influenced by hormones (internal, biological factors), the food that people eat and the exercise that they undertake (external, environmental factors) are also very important influences. So, even if both of our parents are six feet tall and can run fast, we may not grow to fulfil our potential if we are malnourished and take no exercise during our childhood and adolescence.

▶ Failure to nurture our potential can mean that we lose or never express our abilities

Environmental influences on our physical growth and personal development include our culture, the social groups that we belong to and the physical circumstances in which we live. Poor housing conditions and not enough food to eat are factors associated with poor growth in children, and illness in all age groups. Nurture has a very powerful effect in shaping our social, emotional and intellectual development as well as some influence on our physical growth.

A person's growth and development is influenced by both nature and nurture factors, then. The discussion about which is the more powerful and influential is sometimes called the nature/nurture debate. The only safe conclusion in the nature/nurture debate is that people develop through the combined effects and interaction of nature and nurture. For example, your reading and writing skills will have developed since you were a child because you have learnt and practised them. This sort of development is said to be caused by nurture influences. On the other hand, your body will have developed largely because of nature. You will have grown taller and heavier since you were born because of genetically programmed changes. Human beings aren't genetically programmed to read or write. We have to learn and practise these skills. At the same time we don't have to be taught or practise how to grow taller or heavier.

ACTIVITY

Nature or nurture?

Produce a list of the characteristics you possess that you feel are inherited. (Hint: think about physical features that you have in common with your parents, brothers or sisters.)

Now produce a list of the environmental influences that have played a role in your development. (Hint: think about the important experiences and features of your surroundings that have affected you.)

Types of human growth and development

Within each of the five main life stages, changes occur in our physical, emotional, social, and intellectual characteristics, qualities and abilities.

Physical growth and change

Most of the physical growth and change that people experience is predictable and is part of a natural human process of **ageing**. The process of ageing refers to the ways in which the human body gradually changes over time. Human beings grow and develop physical skills from birth until they experience a peak in their physical ability during adulthood. They then experience a slow, gradual decline in their physical abilities until the point at which they die in old age.

Figure 3.2: Development is a continual process

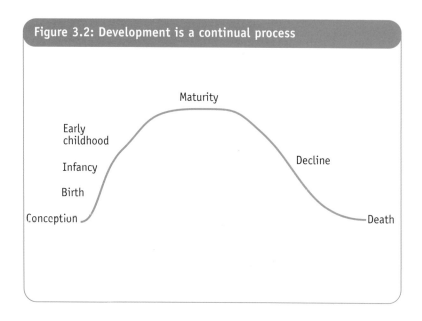

Ageing is mainly influenced by maturation and is a lifelong process. The rate, or speed, at which people age varies. Some very old people retain their energy, mental alertness and enjoyment of life longer than other, much younger, people. The rate at which people age is influenced by a combination of factors. These include the extent to which they inherit 'long life' genes, their attitude to life, health and fitness, and the extent to which they have lived a stressful life.

▶ Exercise is important if we are to stay healthy as we age

Emotional and social development

The emotional and social aspects of personal development begin at birth and are very closely related to each other. These areas of personal development are concerned with people's feelings (emotional) and relationships (social).

Emotions are feelings, like love, happiness, disappointment and anger. We develop and express these through our experience of relationships and social situations. As they go through each life stage, people's emotional development depends on their experiences – particularly how they are treated by other people and how much they learn and mature as a result.

Emotional development involves the:

- growth of feelings about and awareness of self
- growth of feelings towards other people
- development of self-image and identity.

Social development involves the growth of people's relationships with others, the social skills they develop and use in relating to others, and the way in which they learn the culture, or way of life, of the society in which they live.

Intellectual development

You are now able to read books, remember and find what you need when you go shopping, manage your own money, remember your friend's phone numbers and even your assignment deadlines (sometimes)! You might not do all of these things every day but you will perform many similar activities every day of the week. All of these activities rely on your use of intelligence or thinking ability. The term **intellectual development** (sometimes also called **cognitive development**) is used to refer to the way in which thinking, memory and language ability improve and are refined throughout life. Intellectual (cognitive) development is a process that occurs in all human life stages.

A few centuries ago it was believed that children were born with a mind that was like a blank book. It was assumed that the book was gradually filled with knowledge and information gained from what the child experienced in the environment. This view is no longer as popular or widely held as it once was. There are now a number of different ways of explaining intellectual development.

Jean Piaget (1896–1980), a Swiss scientist interested in children's development, produced a theory that children are born with some basic abilities and lots of potential that gradually unfolds as they grow older. Piaget thought that intellectual development occurred in four main stages that children move through as they mature. The names of these stages, and the approximate age at which each occurs, are:

▼ It's never too late to learn

Sensorimotor stage	0–2 years
Pre-operational stage	2–7 years
Concrete operational stage	7–11 years
Formal operational stage	11+ years

Further information about the kind of intellectual development that happens in each stage is given in the case studies on pages 169, 182, 187, 194 and 199.

During infancy and childhood our intellectual abilities are said to be maturing. With the help of planned learning experiences in educational settings like school, college and university, and through informal learning from others in work and social situations, our intellectual abilities are nurtured so that we fulfil our potential.

Developmental norms

The sequence and timing of human growth and development tend to follow a generally predictable pattern. Expected human growth and development milestones, and the points in a person's life when they happen, are commonly referred to as **developmental norms**. However, whilst there is a generally expected pattern of human growth and development, it is important that you don't think of this as an exact timetable that 'normal' people follow. This interpretation is not true. A child, teenager or adult is not abnormal if he or she reaches growth and developmental milestones at slightly different times to those suggested by developmental norms. His or her development, if it is faster or slower than the norm, may be different to the expected pattern for a variety of reasons. The general pattern of human development is described in the life stage case studies that appear throughout this unit.

Build your learning

Summary points

- Human growth and development is a lifelong process.

- People experience physical, intellectual, emotional and social development and change throughout their lives.

- Human growth and development follows a pattern that can be divided into five main life stages.

- Growth and development are both affected by nature (internal) and nurture (external) influences.

Key words and phrases

You should know the meaning of the words and phrases listed below as they relate to basic ideas about the types of development. If you are not sure about them, go back through the last six pages to refresh your understanding.

- **Development**
- **Growth**
- **Life span**
- **Life stage**
- **Maturation**
- **Nature**
- **Nurture**
- **Ageing**
- **Developmental norms**
- **Emotions**
- **Intellectual development**
- **Social development**
- **Cognitive development**

Student questions

1 Explain what growth and development each mean and how you would distinguish between them.

2 Name one influence of nature on growth and development.

3 Identify an example of the influence of nurture on growth and development.

4 What kind of abilities improve during intellectual development?

5 What are developmental norms?

CASE STUDY

Life stage: Infancy

Brendan O'Brien is a three-year-old boy, born and brought up in London. He lives with his parents, older sister and grandmother. Brendan currently goes to a playgroup twice a week at the local community centre.

Physical development

Immediately after he was born, and then five minutes later, the midwife checked Brendan's physical condition using the Apgar score method (see Figure 3.3). Brendan was born with a number of basic **physical reflexes** (see Figure 3.4). For example, as soon as he was born he could breathe, blink his eyes, distinguish colours and smells and suck when something was pushed into his mouth.

During infancy Brendan grew very rapidly. By the age of one he weighed three times his birth weight, was one and a half times as tall, had a comparatively smaller head and a more solid physical frame than when he was born. He also developed some basic **motor skills** during his first year of life. At first Brendan couldn't even hold his head up or reach out for things close to him. In the first few weeks and months of life he developed basic forms of movement, such as holding his head up and moving his arms and legs. During his first year Brendan was gradually able to hold his head up for longer periods of time, started to reach out for things he could see, and began to crawl.

Emotional and social development

In his first year of life Brendan had a small circle of people to whom he was attached. His parents, sister and grandmother were the people who cared for him and with whom he spent most of his time. These people provided Brendan with the basic security and safety from which he was able to explore the world around him. By the age of six months, Brendan's bonding with Fiona and Gerry, his parents and main carers, had become very strong. Brendan, like most babies, became very distressed when he was separated from his parents at this point in his life.

Intellectual development

Like a lot of parents, Brendan's mum and dad were surprised and excited by the speed and ways in which Brendan's intellectual development progressed. At birth, Brendan was able to respond to light and sound in a very simple way. Brendan's mum said that he could recognise her face, and smiled at her, when he was three months old. His dad can remember how he gradually made more noise, especially when he was wet or hungry, and could say 'dada' by the time he was nine months old.

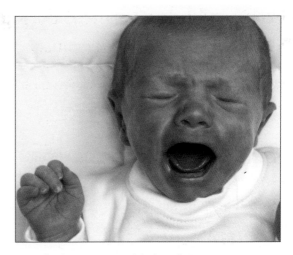

Brendan's parents said that he was a very curious child, always keen to touch and play with toys, especially those that made a noise! By the age of one Brendan had learnt to recognise his own name and responded to simple words like 'good', 'no' and 'well done'. He was gradually learning new words. His first words after 'dada' and 'mama' were 'dog' and 'car'. In his second and third year Brendan's use of language increased dramatically. By the time he was three, Brendan could hold a simple conversation with any member of his family and had developed a habit of asking a lot of questions!

Figure 3.3: Apgar score

Observation	Score given		
	0	1	2
Heart rate	Absent	<100/min	>100/min
Respiratory rate	No breathing	Weak cry and shallow breathing	Strong cry and regular breathing
Muscle tone	Flaccid	Some flexion of extremities	Well flexed
Response to stimulation	None	Some motion of feet	Cry
Colour	'Blue'; poor	Body okay, extremities 'blue'	Good colour all over

Growth and development during infancy
Physical growth and development

Physical growth is very rapid and significant during infancy. The physical changes that children experience during this stage of their life transform their appearance and provide a basis for the intellectual, social and emotional development that also occurs. Physical change during infancy is influenced by a number of factors.

▲ A baby who is rapidly growing and developing

Influences on growth

Both nature and nurture influences are responsible for the physical growth and development that a child experiences during infancy. However, the human body is programmed to mature naturally. Because of the maturation process, all babies move through the same sequence of physical growth and

---

Figure 3.4: The reflexes of newborn babies

Placing

stimulus: brushing the top of foot against table top

response: the baby lifts its foot and places it on a hard surface

Sucking

stimulus: placing nipple or teat into the mouth

response: the baby sucks

Moro (startle)

stimulus: insecure handling or sudden loud noise

response: the baby throws head; the fingers fan out; the arms return to the embrace posture and the baby cries

Grasping

stimulus: placing object in baby's palm

response: fingers close tightly around the object

Rooting

stimulus: brushing the cheek with a finger or nipple

response: the baby turns to the side of stimulus

Walking

stimulus: held standing, feet touching a hard surface

response: the baby moves its legs forward alternately and walks development changes, even though as individual babies they do so at different speeds. The physical characteristics that Brendan inherited from his parents' chromosomes were prompted to gradually unfold by hormonal messages.

Brendan's pattern of growth and development during this life stage was also nurtured by his parents who gave him a balanced diet and plenty of opportunities to use his developing body in play and other physical daily activities.

Hormone growth messages

Hormones are natural chemicals produced by glands in different parts of the body. The testes, ovaries and pituitary glands produce hormones that act as chemical messengers, promoting growth that affects body shape and size.

Patterns of development

The changes in physical appearance and ability that Brendan experienced in the early months of his life unfolded in a particular pattern. Change occurred from his head downwards and from the middle of his body outwards (see Figure 3.5). This is the same for all babies who follow developmental norms.

Brendan's physical development clearly followed this pattern. For example, he was able to hold his head up without help before he could use his body to sit up. After this he was able

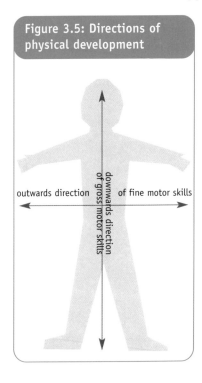

Figure 3.5: Directions of physical development

outwards direction of fine motor skills

downwards direction of gross motor skills

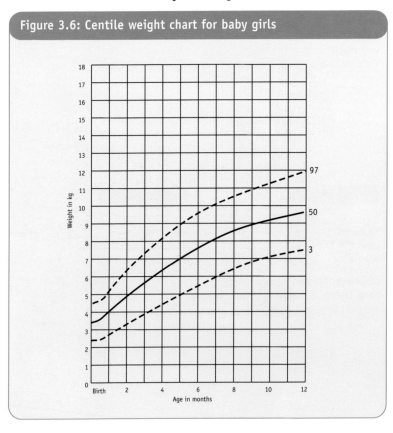

Figure 3.6: Centile weight chart for baby girls

Weight in kg

Age in months

97

50

3

to use his legs to crawl. During infancy Brendan's bones gradually grew and hardened, and his muscles grew stronger, in the same head downwards, middle outwards pattern. This enabled him to carry out new sorts of movement as his body underwent physical development and change. Brendan's mother Fiona recorded the timing of his 'motor milestones' in a baby book that she kept (see Figure 3.8).

Measuring physical change

It is possible to check whether a child's physical development is within the normal range of what is expected. As we saw in Unit 2, centile charts are commonly used to compare a child's pattern of growth to the average growth rates of children of the same age. Centile charts of weight and height have been compiled after studying and recording the growth patterns of thousands of children to work out average and expected patterns. There are different charts for girls and boys. When they are filled in for a specific child, centile charts present clear, visual information on growth.

The bold line on the chart in Figure 3.6 represents the average measure of growth in weight expected in female babies over the first twelve months of their life. This means that if a five-month-old girl weighs 7 kg, on average 50 per cent of girls

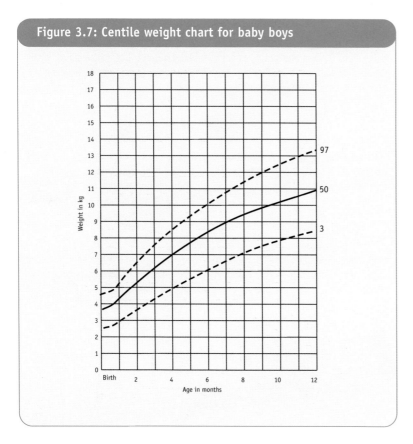

Figure 3.7: Centile weight chart for baby boys

Figure 3.8: Brendan's baby book

BRENDAN'S BABY BOOK	AGE	PHYSICAL	EMOTIONAL
	1 month	Holds his head up for a few seconds! Eyes follow moving light.	Cries when he's hungry and thirsty.
	3 months	Can kick vigorously. Eyes follow people when they move.	Enjoys being cuddled and played with. Cries for his mum when she leaves him.
	6 months	Can support himself on his wrists. Turns to whoever is speaking.	Anxious with strangers. Becomes angry and frustrated. Likes to be with his mum the most!
	9 months	Trying to stand. Looks at himself in the mirror. Can sit without support.	Knows his family. Still anxious about strangers. Can be irritable if his routine is altered.
	12 months	Pulls himself up to a standing position. Uses his fingers to eat. Can walk without assistance.	Shows affection, kissing and cuddling his sister. Likes to see familiar faces but is less worried about strangers.
	18 months	Walks well. Pushes and pulls his toys about. Can walk upstairs but creeps backwards downstairs!	Affectionate, but still reserved with strangers. Likes to see familiar faces.
	2 years	Can run. Likes to climb on furniture and throw his ball. Learning to ride his first tricycle.	Has become moody. Wants his mum all the time. Has temper tantrums when he doesn't get his way. Plays beside other children at nursery but not with them.
	2.5 years	Very active. Runs and climbs and can jump from a low step with his feet together.	Very dependent on his mum and dad. Doesn't want to share his toys with other children.
	3 years	Likes to sit with his feet crossed at the ankles. Can walk upstairs properly without help.	Less moody and more affectionate with his sister. Started sharing toys at nursery.

INTELLECTUAL	SOCIAL
Interested in sounds.	Sleeps most of the day and night. Stops crying when picked up or spoken to.
Knows his mum and shows excitement! Can listen, hold a toy and smile.	Responds happily to his dad and becomes excited at bath and meal times.
Reacts to speech and makes a noise himself. Uses his eyes a lot. Holds toys and explores using hands. Listens to sounds.	Puts everything in his mouth! Plays with his hands and feet. He's trying to hold his bottle when feeding.
Tries to talk in a 'babbling' way. Says 'mama' and 'dada'. Shouts for attention and understands 'no'!	Plays 'peek a boo' with his sister. Imitates hand clapping. Puts his hands around his feeding cup.
Knows his own name! Obeys simple instructions and can say a few words of his own.	Can drink from his cup without help. Holds a spoon but can't feed himself. Likes finding hidden toys!
Can say 6–20 recognisable words. Talks a lot more. Repeats the last word of short sentences. Enjoys and tries to join in with nursery rhymes. Likes looking at picture books and scribbles on paper. Seems to be left-handed.	Can hold his spoon and get food into his mouth. Gives his cup back when he's finished! Can take off his shoes and socks. Says when he want to go to the toilet.
Can talk more and uses about 50 words. Understands people talking to him. Uses his own name and wants to know the names of objects and other people. Likes to build towers of six or seven cubes. He is definitely left-handed.	Asks for food and a drink. Uses his spoon without spilling anything. Knows how to put his own shoes on.
Talks a lot. Asks questions all the time, likes stories and looking at his picture books. Knows himself in photographs.	Uses a spoon and sometimes a fork. Usually dry during the day.
Knows his full name, sex and how old he is. Has simple conversations and is constantly asking questions. Demands to hear his favourite story over and over again. Can count to ten, copy a simple shape and name colours.	Eats with a fork and a spoon and has many friends at nursery.

of the same age will weigh less than her and 50 per cent of girls of the same age will weigh more than her. If a girl weighs 12 kg at 12 months, then the graph says that 97 per cent of girls of the same age will weigh less than she does and 3 per cent will, on average, weigh more.

By recording a child's growth on centile charts, care workers such as health visitors and GPs, can monitor progress and note whether growth is proceeding in an expected pattern.

Identifying early milestones

Talk to a parent who has a child under the age of five. Ask him or her to identify the age at which the child first carried out each of the following actions.

- Smiled
- Said his or her first word
- Said his or her first sentence
- Was able to remember and say his or her own name
- Slept through the night without waking
- Was dry throughout the night
- Was dry throughout the day
- Walked without help
- Crawled
- Sat up without support
- Jumped without falling over
- Showed a preference for using one hand or the other
- Built a tower of three bricks
- Began to understand sharing

Find out whether the parent feels that his or her child achieved anything unusually early or later than might be expected. Check this against the expected time for achieving this action and decide whether the parent is correct or not.

Emotional and social development

People's early emotional and social development plays an important part in their future relationships and their behaviour towards others. Children like Brendan O'Brien should ideally develop feelings of trust and security early on in their lives. The process through which this occurs is known as attachment. This occurs when a child develops a strong emotional link with his or her parents or main caregivers. The parental response to this emotional linking is known as bonding. Attachment and bonding provide the emotional link between baby and adult through which a first relationship is built.

The quality of the bond is influenced by four things:

- how sensitively the mother understands and responds to the baby's needs
- the personality of the mother
- the consistency of the care that the baby receives
- the baby's own temperament.

Emotional and social development during infancy is extremely important. Like Brendan, children tend to gradually increase their social relationships by including brothers, sisters, relatives and perhaps neighbour's children in their social circle. The nature of the social contacts that children have at this stage are influenced by their emerging communication skills. Children are increasingly able to look at the world from the point of view of other people as they progress through infancy. This is demonstrated by the gradual changes that occur in the way in which children in this age group, like Brendan, play (see Figure 3.9).

Successful social relationships among children are helped by:

- secure attachment in their early years
- opportunities to mix with other children, especially where they involve activities that require cooperation
- the personality of the child – children who are friendly, supportive and optimistic make friends more easily than children who are negative and aggressive.

Intellectual development

Intellectual development involves changes in a person's thinking, memory and language abilities. It is a process of change that begins as soon as a person is born and never really ends until death. Infancy is a life stage when a great deal of basic intellectual development happens.

Figure 3.9: Stages of play

0–1 year: solo play

"It's difficult for me to think of people other than myself so I like to play on my own. I learn through exploring everything around me."

2–3 years: parallel play

"I'm still mainly interested in myself and I can't see the sense of sharing yet. I am interested in other people so I like to be near them. I learn by imitating other people."

3 years old: associative play

"I'm beginning to understand how they feel and to be sympathetic, so that makes it easier to play with other children. I learn a lot by imitating and pretending to be people who are important to me."

Over 3 years old: cooperative play

"I can see that it's important to share and help other children. I realise that if I cooperate with the other children we have more fun and do more interesting things."

Influences on development

Intellectual development during infancy is mainly a matter of maturing. It is generally thought that infants are born with the capacity to learn, think and use language and that the environment in which they live influences the speed and extent to which they develop intellectually. Intellectual ability during this life stage is therefore said to be a matter of both nature and nurture.

As an infant Brendan O'Brien saw and experienced a large number of things for the first time in his life. Young children like Brendan are very quick to use these new experiences to acquire a better understanding of the world around them.

Stage of development

Jean Piaget, the Swiss scientist who had an interest in child development, identified a number of stages of intellectual development, with the first beginning in infancy. He saw infancy as the time when children went through what he called the sensorimotor stage of intellectual development. This stage is said to occur between birth and two years of age. During this stage babies learn and absorb a lot about themselves and the world through their senses (touch, hearing, sight, smell, taste – hence sensori) and through physical activity (also known as motor activity). One very important lesson that children learn during this stage is that objects and people in the world continue to exist even when they can't be seen. This might seem obvious to you now, but it's not to a young baby. In early infancy, before eight months, children won't search for a hidden object as it no longer seems to 'exist' but will do so in later infancy as they develop what is known as object permanence.

Language development

A second key feature of intellectual development during infancy is learning the basics of a spoken language. Caregivers responsible for young children have an important role to play in helping them to communicate well and to use language in a wide variety of ways. While children do not actually use their first proper words until they are about one year old, babies are developing communication skills almost straight from birth.

The initial communications of babies are in the form of smiles, movements and noises that are part of a 'conversation' with a caregiver. The baby is already able to give and receive information and to communicate feelings. Young children move rapidly through the different stages of language development, from babbling at 8–10 months, to their first words between one and two years of age, to short sentences from 18 months. By two and a half, children are learning a few new words a day, so that by three they have a vocabulary of about a thousand words.

Although children can talk effectively by the time they are three, it is not correct to think that language development ends there. Language learning continues throughout childhood and people continue to refine their use of language throughout life.

Build your learning

Summary points

- Infancy is the first stage of life span development.

- Physical growth and development are very rapid during infancy, with the child significantly increasing in size and developing many basic physical skills.

- Significant intellectual, emotional and social development occurs during infancy as the child experiences new aspects of the world and tries to make sense of them.

- Maturation is a natural developmental process that begins during infancy, with physical and intellectual changes gradually unfolding.

- A variety of environmental, or 'nurture', factors also influence the speed and pattern of growth and development during infancy.

Key words and phrases

You should know the meaning of the words and phrases listed below as they relate to growth and development during infancy.

- **Physical reflexes**
- **Motor skills**
- **Hormones**
- **Centile charts**
- **Attachment**
- **Bonding**
- **Maturation**
- **Sensorimotor stage**

Student questions

1 Name three physical reflexes that a child is born with.

2 What are motor skills?

3 In your own words, explain how a child's physical growth is measured during infancy.

4 Why are attachment and bonding felt to be important developmental processes?

5 How does an infant learn about the world during the sensorimotor stage of intellectual development?

ASSESSMENT WORK

Describing the physical characteristics of infancy

Infancy is the first life stage, when babies experience rapid physical growth and development. This activity gives you an opportunity to produce work that demonstrates your knowledge and understanding of physical growth and development during infancy. The work that you do here will become a part of your unit assignment.

	Assessment criteria	Which tasks do I need to do?
Pass	Accurately illustrate human development by describing the physical characteristics of different life stages.	1a 1b 1c

What to do

1a Obtain information on physical development during infancy. There are lots of books that you can use as a resource for this. You might also want to use pictures (photocopies, photographs or your own drawings) to illustrate your work.

1b Decide what the key features of infant physical development are. Concentrate on describing the different ways in which babies change physically between birth and three years of age.

1c Put your work together in such a way that it can later form a section of your end of unit report on human development.

Key skills

C2.2, C2.3, IT2.1, IT2.2, IT2.3, N2.1, N2.3

It may be possible to claim these key skills for this coursework depending on how you have completed the tasks and presented your work. Your teacher will need to check your evidence against the key skills specification.

You do not have to base your work on a real child. You can give a general explanation of physical growth and development during infancy. You can base your work on a real child if you get permission from his or her parents (and ideally from the child). If you can get permission, you might want to include (again with permission) photographs of the child which illustrate key physical changes.

181

CASE STUDY

Life stage: Early childhood

Emma O'Brien is Brendan's sister. She attends primary school where she has a lot of friends. Emma is learning to swim and is looking forward to going to the seaside for a summer holiday.

Physical growth and development

Between the ages of four to six years Emma learnt to run, jump, hop and ride a bicycle. She enjoys playing ball and skipping games and is now a very active, energetic child. Emma's physical appearance has changed a lot during the last few years. She has become less top heavy than she was as an infant as she's lost her baby fat and has become more physically coordinated, stronger and able to move in more subtle and sophisticated ways.

During the next few years Emma's muscle tissue will increase and she will become taller, stronger and more robust. She will develop much more distinct physical features than in the previous phase. By her late childhood Emma will have developed facial features that will change very little throughout her adult life. Her physical growth will progress slowly and gradually in this phase until puberty begins in about her twelfth year.

Social and emotional development

During her early childhood Emma has faced a number of social and emotional challenges. Going to school was a major event in Emma's life. It meant being with other children, making new friendships and listening to people who were not her parents or close family members. Emma found this difficult to begin with but now enjoys going to school. In this stage of her childhood Emma began to acquire new communication skills (language and listening) and social behaviours and used these to build relationships with a broad range of people, including new friends and school staff. Emma's social world expanded rapidly after she started going to school.

Intellectual development

In her first year at primary school, Emma began to organise her thinking more. She was keen to learn new things and participate in class activities. Emma's speech quickly became more sophisticated as she learnt more words and improved her ways of using them. At school Emma learnt how to read and write and developed the ability to think about and work out her own solutions to simple problems and frustrations that she faced.

Growth and development during early childhood

Physical growth and development

Have you been to a primary school recently? If so you might have noticed that learning activities in reception and early infants classes are often directed towards refining and expanding the coordination and **fine motor skills** that young children begin to develop at this stage in their lives. Emma was able to do many of the physical activities described in the case study because she passed rapidly through the stage of physical development where her balance control improved.

Social and emotional development

During early childhood the developmental problems faced by children like Brendan and Emma are related to their need to develop relationships with children and adults outside their close family. It is at this time that children first leave their parents to go to school. This broadens their relationships and expands their social world but it can be emotionally difficult. You may still remember how you felt when your parents left you at the school gate on your first day at school and went home without you! The first days at primary school are very distressing for some children.

During this life stage children have to learn to cooperate, communicate and spend time with a new set of adults and children. Most children gradually increase their self-confidence and independence during this stage, though a variety of nature and nurture factors influence the extent to which individual children develop their confidence and independence. For example, a child who feels encouraged and supported and who has good role models develops his or her self-confidence and sense of independence more easily than a child who is criticised, discouraged and over protected during his or her early childhood.

▼ Starting school can be an unsettling experience for some children

Intellectual development

The second stage of intellectual development in Piaget's theory (see page 167) is called the **pre-operational stage**. This is said to occur between the ages of two and seven years. In this stage, children like Emma O'Brien are less reliant on physical learning (seeing, touching and holding things) because they develop the ability to think about them when the objects are not actually there. Nevertheless children's thinking in this life stage is still limited. They still tend to think about everything from their own point of view and are not aware that others may have different viewpoints. This is known as **egocentrism**.

Moral development

During early childhood an important change occurs in children's sense of values and in the way that they think. A child's conscience, the ability to decide what is good or bad and to distinguish between right and wrong in his or her own and other people's behaviour, is said to develop through three stages.

At first children tend to base their judgements about right and wrong on rules that they have been taught by people who have authority in their lives, such as parents and teachers. During early childhood children generally conform to rules if this means that they will avoid being punished or that they will receive rewards. The standards of morality that are taught or demonstrated by parents tend to have a big influence on young children who wish to be a good boy or girl. This lasts until they reach adolescence, when making moral judgements becomes a more sophisticated process.

▲ Learning to work out problems

▼ A person's conscience develops from early childhood

Build your learning

Summary points

- Children develop new physical skills and grow heavier and taller during childhood, but the rate of growth is slower than it was during infancy.

- Intellectual, emotional and social changes become more significant areas of development during early childhood.

- Going to school, making friends with other children and meeting more adults are all important influences on intellectual, emotional and social development during childhood.

- Nature (internal maturation) and nurture (environmental) factors continue to influence growth and development during childhood.

- Children begin to develop their conscience by learning and applying rules about what is right and wrong.

Key words and phrases

You should know the meaning of the words and phrases listed below as they relate to growth and development during infancy.

- **Fine motor skills**
- **Egocentrism**
- **Pre-operational stage**
- **Moral development**

Student questions

1 Name some of the environmental factors that are said to stimulate social development during childhood.

2 How can a child's self-confidence and independence be nurtured?

3 Young children are said to be egocentric. What does this mean?

4 Why is the first day at school distressing for some children?

5 What role do adults play in a child's early moral development?

ASSESSMENT WORK

Describing the physical characteristics of childhood

Childhood is the second life stage. Children continue to grow and develop physically, but not at the same rapid rate as when they were infants. This assessment preparation activity is very like the one that you completed on page 181. You are asked to produce some work on physical growth and development during childhood that can be used in your unit assignment.

	Assessment criteria	Which tasks do I need to do?
Pass	Accurately illustrate human development by describing the physical characteristics of different life stages.	2a 2b 2c

By carrying out this work now you will reduce the amount of assignment work that you will have to do at the end of the unit.

Key skills

C2.2, C2.3, IT2.1, IT2.2, IT2.3, N2.1, N2.3

It may be possible to claim these key skills for this coursework depending on how you have completed the tasks and presented your work. Your teacher will need to check your evidence against the key skills specification.

What to do

2a Obtain information on physical development during childhood. There are lots of books that you can use as a resource for this. You might also want to use pictures (photocopies, photographs or your own drawings) to illustrate your work.

2b Decide which key features of childhood physical development you want to cover. Again, concentrate on describing the different ways in which children physically change during their childhood (5–12 years).

2c Put your work together in such a way that it can later form a section of your end of unit report on human development.

You do not have to base your work on a real child. You can give a general explanation of physical growth and development during childhood. You can base your work on a real child if you get permission from his or her parents (and ideally also from the child). If you can get permission to do this you might want to include (again with permission) photographs of the child which illustrate key physical changes.

CASE STUDY

Life stage: Puberty and adolescence

Emma O'Brien is now eight years old and settled at school. She will enter puberty in the next four or five years.

Physical growth and development

When Emma enters puberty she is likely to experience a growth spurt in which her body grows and changes very rapidly. Emma's puberty will also involve the development of secondary sexual characteristics. This will begin with the growth of pubic hair and Emma's breasts will begin to develop. She will also experience further growth of her uterus and vagina, widening of her hips and the onset of her menstrual cycle.

Like most boys, Brendan O'Brien is not likely to experience an adolescent growth spurt and significant physical change until he reaches the age of 13. When this happens the first indication of puberty is likely to be the growth of his testes, scrotum and pubic hair. Brendan will grow body hair (on his face and chest and in his armpits) and his voice will get deeper. Brendan will grow to his maximum height and develop greater muscle bulk.

Emotional and social development

When Emma begins to progress through adolescence, she will experience a period of major emotional change and social development. When she reaches adulthood, her parents, like those of many other people, will probably look back and say that they had most problems with her during this life stage! Emotions and relationships can feel intense and be difficult for many adolescents to manage.

Emma will expand her social circle and her friends, or **peer group**, will become more important to her. She will try to break free from the authority of her parents and seek to be much more independent. Like most adolescent girls, Emma will begin to look for a partner. Experimenting with intimate relationships, whether they involve sexual activity or not, will lead Emma to experience the positive and negative emotions that can result from close relationships. Socially and emotionally, adolescence is likely to be an exciting, and at times difficult, life stage for Emma. Her search for **identity** and independence will bring her into conflict with her parents, teachers and friends at times. It should also lead her to achieve greater self-confidence and a sense of who she is, the sort of friends she prefers and the kind of partner she is seeking.

Intellectual development

Emma will attend secondary school and take public examinations, such as GCSEs and GNVQs during adolescence. She will learn a lot of new skills, develop her knowledge of different subjects and be required to remember and think about a huge amount of information during this time. The way that Emma thinks will change from the way that she thought during childhood. She is likely to develop the ability to use abstract thinking and may doubt, and rebel against, the rules that her parents taught her about what is good and bad, right and wrong. Intellectual development during adolescence will enable Emma to question what she is told and she will begin to develop a sense of her own values.

Growth and development during adolescence

Adolescence begins at about the age of 12 and ends somewhere between 16 and 22. This stage of maturation is called **puberty**. In terms of physical growth and change, emotional and social development and intellectual development, adolescence is a very active phase. The onset of puberty is the beginning of a significant process of change in physical growth and personal development.

You will have noticed that in the adolescence life stage case study we talked about how Emma and Brendan O'Brien would grow and develop in the future. It is possible to do this because individual development follows a relatively predictable pattern. You might remember that we called this normal development earlier in this unit (see page 168). One stage of development that most readers of this book will have recent experience of is adolescence. In the next section we will try to explain the growth and development changes that occur during puberty.

Physical growth and change

The growth spurt and physical changes that occur in puberty are caused by an increase in the activity of **hormones**. Hormones are chemical secretions that pass directly into the blood from the endocrine glands.

Figure 3.10: Location of the endocrine glands in the body

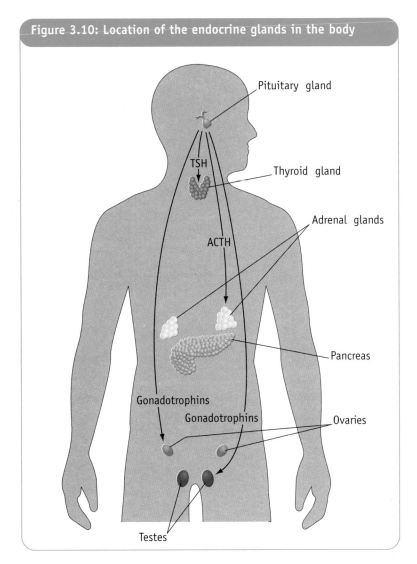

The two main glands that secrete the hormones which affect growth and development are the thyroid gland and the pituitary gland. Several different hormones are secreted by each of these glands (see Figure 3.11).

The pituitary gland is only the size of a pea but it is very important in controlling the hormone production that affects growth and development. The pituitary gland is located at the base of the brain.

The **thyroid gland** is located in the neck. It too has an important influence on general growth rate, bone and muscle development and in the function of the reproductive organs. During puberty the testes in boys produce the hormone **testosterone** and the ovaries in girls produce **oestrogen** and **progesterone**. These are hormones that that control the development and function of the reproductive organs.

Figure 3.11: Hormones secreted by pituitary and thyroid glands		
Gland	**Hormone**	**Function/effect**
Pituitary	Prolactin	Stimulates milk production by mammary glands.
	Growth hormone	Stimulates general body growth.
	Lipotropin	Increases the rate of use of stored fat.
	Gonad-stimulating hormone	Regulates the development of reproductive organs.
Thyroid	Thyroxine	Controls the rate of growth and the rate at which glucose is used to release energy.

Emotional and social development

In terms of social and emotional development, puberty and adolescence can be a difficult, and very active, time. The need for an individual identity and a sense of social and emotional belonging are important concerns in this phase. Adolescents usually experiment with intimate, personal relationships with members of the opposite sex, and sometimes the same sex, as they explore their sexuality and the positive and negative emotions that result from close relationships. This experimentation can include making decisions about whether or not to engage in sexual activity as a part of an intimate, personal relationship. In this phase of social and emotional development, individuals tend to gain greater understanding of the thoughts, feelings and motives of others.

Intellectual development

Intellectual development during adolescence mainly involves the emergence of **abstract thinking**. A person who can think abstractly can think about things that aren't actually there and things that don't actually exist. This sounds a bit odd but it is probably a feature of your own thinking that you now take for granted. For example, algebra equations involve abstract thinking and so does thinking about the beginning of the universe. However, imagining what it would be like to be stranded on an tropical island with your favourite film or television star might be a more enjoyable way of testing whether you can think abstractly! Abstract thinking is considered to be the final stage of thought development. An important outcome of intellectual development during adolescence is that young people's values become increasingly consistent. Intellectual development is not completed in adolescence however, and continues throughout life.

Moral development

During adolescence the way that people think about moral issues, such as right and wrong, changes. During adolescence individuals typically base their judgements about right and wrong on the rules, or norms, of the social groups to which they belong. These include family, friendship and peer groups, churches and clubs. However, whereas children believe that good behaviour is what pleases important individuals in their lives, adolescents tend to be guided by the more abstract laws and rules of society. Adolescents are more likely to be guided by a sense of duty to conform to the general rules of the social groups to which they belong rather than obeying the specific things that their parents tell them. Being law abiding and a good citizen is more important than being a good boy or girl.

 Build your learning

Summary points

- A physical growth spurt occurs during adolescence. This results in rapid growth in size and changes in body shape and physical ability.

- The term puberty is used to describe the physical changes, particularly the development of sexual characteristics, which occur during this life stage.

- Physical change during adolescence is largely controlled by the activity of hormones.

- Adolescence is a period of rapid emotional and social development in which relationships with non-family members become increasingly important.

- A significant feature of intellectual development during adolescence is the emergence of abstract thinking.

- Adolescents think about moral issues in a more sophisticated way than younger children.

Key words and phrases

You should know the meaning of the words and phrases listed below as they relate to growth and development during adolescence. If you are not sure about any of them, go back through the last four pages to check and refresh your understanding.

- Puberty
- Secondary sexual characteristics
- Hormones
- Pituitary gland

- Thyroid gland
- Testosterone
- Oestrogen
- Progesterone

- Abstract thinking
- Thyroxine
- Peer group
- Identity

Student questions

1 Describe some of the key physical changes that occur during adolescence.

2 Name the new type of thinking ability that many adolescents develop and explain what it involves.

3 Explain how two important factors affect growth and development during puberty. You should choose one nature and one nurture factor.

4 What reasons can you give to explain why individuals come into conflict with their parents more during adolescence than in childhood?

5 Is a person's way of judging moral issues likely to change during adolescence? Explain your answer.

ASSESSMENT WORK

Describing the physical characteristics of adolescence

Adolescence is the third life stage. As part of the unit assignment you are asked to demonstrate your knowledge and understanding of the physical characteristics of adolescence.

Assessment criteria		Which tasks do I need to do?
Pass	Accurately illustrate human development by describing the physical characteristics of different life stages.	

If you carry out the activities now you will have completed part of the work needed for your end of unit assignment.

What to do

3a Obtain information on physical development during adolescence. There are lots of books (like this one!) that you can use as a resource for this and you should have some personal experience to draw on! You might want to use pictures (photocopies, photographs or your own drawings) to illustrate your work.

3b Decide which key features of adolescent physical development you want to cover. Concentrate on describing the different ways in which individuals change physically during adolescence.

3c Put your work together in such a way that it can later form a section of your end of unit report on human development.

You do not have to base your work on a real teenager. If you do use a friend or relative as a source of examples get his or her permission and make sure that he or she is happy for you to use any photographs of him or her.

Key skills

C2.2, C2.3, IT2.1, IT2.2, IT2.3, N2.1, N2.3

It may be possible to claim these key skills for this coursework depending on how you have completed the tasks and presented your work. Your teacher will need to check your evidence against the key skills specification.

CASE STUDY

Life stage: Adulthood

Gerry and Fiona O'Brien have been married for eight years. Both were born and brought up in Manchester. Gerry and Fiona came to live in London six years ago. Gerry is a specialist orthopaedic doctor and works in the National Health Service. Fiona works part time as a primary school teacher.

Physical growth and development

Physically, both Gerry and Fiona are in the prime of their lives. At 30 years old, Fiona is in the first half of early adulthood. Gerry is 40 and is in the second half of early adulthood. Fiona and Gerry have produced two children and can have more children until Fiona experiences the menopause in later adulthood. They would like one more child to complete their family.

Gerry and Fiona are fit and healthy at this point in their lives. Fiona is a keen swimmer and says that her strength, speed and stamina when swimming are the best they've ever been. Gerry likes to go jogging but says that he is no longer as fast, or as light, as he once was. Gerry has recently started to lose some of his hair and predicts that he will go bald, like his father, by the time he is fifty years old!

Emotional and social development

Developing a close intimate relationship, getting married and having children has fundamentally altered Fiona and Gerry's lives over the last eight years. They are very committed to their role as parents, though both are also keen to develop their careers and currently enjoy their jobs. Work, children and marriage will be the key influences on Fiona and Gerry's social and emotional development during adulthood. Their circle of friends, ambitions and emotional life are all likely to be focused on successfully raising their family, succeeding at work and developing their relationship.

Intellectual development

Fiona is a qualified primary school teacher and Gerry is a qualified doctor. Both are continuing to develop their careers by taking courses and learning about new developments in their fields of work. Gerry has been a orthopaedic doctor for six years and makes use of his specialist training and experience when he sees new clients. In their leisure time Fiona and Gerry both enjoy reading, watching films, going to museums and travelling abroad on holiday. At this stage in their lives Fiona and Gerry are learning a lot of new things and are using their learning, intellectual abilities and experience in their everyday lives.

Growth and development during adulthood

Adulthood is the life stage which people commonly think of, and refer to, as the one where individuals are grown up. If you look back at the diagram of the development process (see Figure 3.2, page 165), you will see that adulthood is, in some ways, the high point of human development. It is the developmental stage at which people have achieved their maximum physical size and capacity and the stage at which their intellectual abilities are at their peak. In this section we try to explain and make sense of the different features of adult growth and development described in the case study.

Physical growth and development

Physical changes in adulthood are not like the changes that occur in childhood and adolescence as they are not about improvement. Growth is largely complete by the end of adolescence. By the time a person reaches adulthood he or she is grown up. People in their early twenties to early thirties are capable of achieving their maximum physical performance during this stage of their life. You may have noticed that most athletes and sports professionals achieve their best performances whilst they are young adults.

In the second half of this phase, from about 30 to 42, adults like Gerry, who is 40, experience an increase in the amount of fatty tissue in their bodies, move more slowly and take longer to recover from their efforts. Men can also start to lose their hair or go grey and women start to get wrinkles around their eyes as their skin becomes less supple.

When Gerry and Fiona reach the middle of their life span, sometime from their forties to late fifties, they will undergo a lot of physical change. During this later phase of adulthood many people experience diminishing abilities and a decline in physical performance compared to earlier stages of their life. The physical changes that human beings experience during adulthood and old age are often referred to as ageing. The physical effects of the ageing process can most clearly be seen by contrasting the physical condition, appearance and abilities of a person during early adulthood and then in old age.

The role of hormones

Both men and women experience the loss of their ability to reproduce during late adulthood. In men this occurs gradually as their levels of testosterone gradually decline throughout adulthood. The more well-known physical change is the one which affects women. Menopause, or the ending of menstruation and the ability to produce children, occurs because a woman's ovaries produce less and less of the hormones oestrogen and progesterone until a point is reached at which the ovaries stop producing eggs.

Emotional and social development

Because of the huge diversity of experience among people in this phase it is difficult to generalise about what happens in terms of social and emotional development. During adulthood people may experience a number of transitions with emotional and social consequences. Marriage and divorce, parenthood and increasing work responsibility and the loss of elderly parents are all life events that are most likely to be experienced during adulthood. This life stage tends to revolve around people trying to achieve their position in society and their ambitions in life.

Intellectual development

As adults, Gerry and Fiona O'Brien are capable of abstract thought, have memories functioning at their peak and can think very quickly. However, compared to older adults, people in this phase lack experience of the world. In contrast, in later adulthood the capacity for quick, reactive thought begins to slow down and memory starts to become slower. This does not mean that older adults are any less capable, just that they may require more time to perform the same intellectual activities as younger adults. Because older people have a greater breadth and depth of knowledge gained from experience they tend to use this to be more analytical and reflective in their thinking.

Moral development

During adulthood some individuals find that they need to revise their ways of judging right and wrong and making other moral judgements. This happens where people discover that the social rules and laws that they followed in adolescence are inadequate because life is just too complex for simple, clear-cut rules. Some adults develop what is known as principled morality. This means that they tend to make judgements on self-chosen principles. They discover situations where they feel that rules and laws need to be ignored or changed and try to use universal principles like truth, equality and social justice to make their decisions. This way of thinking about moral issues is clearly very different to that of children who apply simple rules to gain the approval of parents and other people.

Build your learning

Summary points

- Physical growth is largely complete by the time people reach adulthood.

- Adulthood is the life stage at which people reach their physical peak and then experience a gradual, slow reduction in physical ability.

- Menopause is a key physical change that all women experience at some point in later adulthood.

- People continue to develop intellectually, socially and emotionally throughout the adult life stage.

Key words and phrases

You should know the meaning of the words and phrases listed below as they relate to growth and development during adulthood. If you are not sure about any of them, go back through the last four pages to check and refresh your understanding.

- **Ovaries**
- **Menopause**
- **Ageing**
- **Reflective thinking**

Student questions

1 What development-related reasons can you give to explain why most athletics records are set by people in early adulthood?

2 What features of ageing begin to emerge in men and women from mid-adulthood onwards?

3 Explain what happens during menopause.

4 Identify a number of factors that affect emotional and social development during adulthood.

5 Can an individual's judgement of moral issues develop further during adulthood?

ASSESSMENT WORK

Describing the physical characteristics of adulthood

Adulthood is the fourth stage in our life cycle sequence. People go through a number of physical changes during this phase. As part of the unit assignment you are asked to demonstrate your knowledge and understanding of the physical characteristics of adults.

Assessment criteria		Which tasks do I need to do?
Pass	Accurately illustrate human development by describing the physical characteristics of different life stages.	4a 4b 4c

If you carry out these activities you will have completed part of the work needed for your end of unit assignment.

Key skills

C2.2, C2.3, IT2.1, IT2.2, IT2.3, N2.1, N2.3

It may be possible to claim these key skills for this coursework depending on how you have completed the tasks and presented your work. Your teacher will need to check your evidence against the key skills specification.

What to do

4a Obtain information on physical development during adulthood. Use books (like this one!) as a resource. You might also ask older friends or relatives what they believe the key physical characteristics of an adult are in comparison to an adolescent or older person, perhaps.

4b Decide which key features of adult physical development you want to cover. Concentrate on describing the different physical characteristics that are typical of adulthood.

4c Put your work together in such a way that it can later form a section of your end of unit report on human development.

As with previous assessment work activities, you do not have to base your work on a real person. If you do use a friend or relative in your work, get permission and make sure that he or she is happy for you to use photographs.

CASE STUDY

Life stage: Old age

Gerry's mother, **Sarah O'Brien**, is 73. She still lives in Manchester, and shares a house with another of her sons and his family.

Physical change

Since her late fifties, Sarah has experienced a number of changes in her appearance. Sarah's skin has become more wrinkled, her hair went grey and then turned white and she has experienced a slight decrease in height. Sarah is still very active but tends to walk more slowly and has less stamina than she used to have. Like most other people at this stage of life, Sarah has also experienced sensory changes as her hearing and sight have deteriorated.

Emotional and social development

Sarah is very proud of all of her grandchildren and says that since the death of her husband Harry last year she has become very close to her son, daughter-in-law and their children with whom she now lives. Sarah tends to be quite reflective, reviewing her achievements and her relationships, when she talks with her family members and friends who visit her at home.

Intellectual change and development

Sarah enjoys reading and plays chess as a hobby. She attends a community centre twice a week to meet up with some of her friends and help out in the crèche. Sarah enjoys telling her grandchildren traditional stories and reading to them.

Growth and development in old age

The process of physical ageing quickens for all people from about the age of 55. By the age of 75, the physical effects of ageing are clearly evident. Old age is a time of diminishing physical capabilities, changing emotional experiences, intellectual interests and social circumstances. Ageing inevitably involves physical change but this doesn't mean that when people reach old age they suddenly become unwell, infirm or in need of care. Many older people are physically healthy and robust.

Ageing is a gradual process that is most recognisable in the physical differences that can be seen between people in adulthood and old age. Less visible social, emotional and intellectual changes also occur during this period. Whilst many, usually young people, view old age in a negative way, the gradual decline in abilities that occurs doesn't necessarily mean that older people have a poor quality of life or are unhappy.

Physical change in old age

During old age people experience physical decline with poorer heart and lung function, muscle wastage, brittle bones and stiff joints. These changes are a part of the normal ageing process

- As the skin becomes less elastic, it loses the thin underlying layer of fat and becomes drier and more fragile. Skin changes include the eventual development of wrinkles.
- Hair usually changes colour, turning grey and then white, becoming finer and thinner at the same time. Many men, and a smaller proportion of women, lose hair from the top of the head.
- Slower mental function tends to occur. The speed at which older people are able to think and respond is generally reduced, but mental capacity and intelligence are not lost. Older people do not become any less intelligent as a result of ageing.
- Hearing tends to deteriorate slowly as people age. Quiet and high pitched sounds (and voices!) become more difficult to hear.
- Sight is affected as people age because the lens in the eye loses its elasticity. The result is that older people find it harder to focus on close objects.
- Weakening of bones, also known as osteoporosis, occurs in old age. Calcium and protein are lost from the bones and older people can become physically frail and experience fractures as a result.
- Reduction in height often occurs as people age because the intervertebral discs in the spine become thinner and the older person's posture becomes bent.

Emotional and social change

Social and emotional development takes on a new importance in the later stages of the life span. Sarah, like many older people, has to try to come to terms with the changes that have occurred in her relationships as her own children have grown

Girl Guide to grandmother: ageing is a process of gradual physical change

up, her husband has died and her circle of friends has reduced. Older people continue to develop and change emotionally as they experience new life events and transitions, such as becoming grandparents and retiring from work. They may also have more leisure time in which to build relationships with friends and family members. However, older people may also experience insecurity and loneliness if their social contacts are reduced by retirement or **bereavement**

Intellectual change in old age

Older people maintain and use their intellectual abilities in much the same ways that adults and middle-aged people do. Both the young-old (60–75) and the old-old (75+) need and enjoy intellectually stimulating activities in their lives. There are many negative ideas about older people's intellectual abilities. While it is true that a minority of older people do develop dementia-related illnesses and have memory problems, the majority of older people do not and can perform the same intellectual activities as younger people, if a little more slowly. People who develop dementia-related illnesses tend to have memory problems, especially in recalling recently acquired information, and they become confused more easily. These types of illnesses also result in sufferers gradually losing speech and other abilities that are controlled by the brain.

Build your learning

Summary points

- Old age is a period of ongoing change and personal development.

- Normal ageing tends to involve a reduction in sensory and physical ability.

- Old age is not necessarily a time of illness and impairment. Older people also live active, happy lives.

- Some health problems, such as osteoporosis, confusion and memory impairment are more likely to be experienced in old age, but only by a small proportion of older people.

- Old age provides many people with new developmental opportunities as their leisure time increases and other work and social responsibilities reduce.

Key words and phrases

You should know the meaning of the words and phrases listed below as they relate to growth and development during adulthood and old age. If you are not sure about any of them, go back through the last three pages to check and refresh your understanding.

- **Sensory changes**
- **Normal ageing process**
- **Osteoporosis**
- **Intervertebral discs**
- **Bereavement**

Student questions

1 Why do wrinkles develop as people grow older?

2 What is osteoporosis and why does it occur?

3 Is it true that people lose some height in old age?

4 Which recent event has had a major effect on Sarah's emotional development?

5 What are the key features of dementia-related illness?

ASSESSMENT WORK

⑤

Describing the physical characteristics of old age

Old age is the final life stage. Everybody who reaches old age will experience some change in their physical capabilities. You are asked to describe the physical characteristics of old age as part of the end of unit assignment.

UNIT THREE WORK ASSESSMENT

	Assessment criteria	Which tasks do I need to do?
Pass	Accurately illustrate human development by describing the physical characteristics of different life stages.	5a 5b 5c

What to do

5a Obtain information on physical change during old age. There are lots of books that you can use as a resource for this. You might also use knowledge gained from older people who are your relatives or people you met on work placement.

5b Decide which physical characteristics of old age you want to cover. Concentrate on describing the different ways in which older people experience physical change.

5c Put your work together in such a way that it can later form a section of your end of unit report on human development.

You do not have to base your work on a real older person. As in the previous assessment work activities you can give a general explanation of physical growth and development during old age. You may want to use a friend or relative as a source of examples in your work. Get his or her permission before doing so and make sure that he or she is happy for you to use any photographs.

Key skills

C2.2, C2.3, IT2.1, IT2.2, IT2.3, N2.1, N2.3

It may be possible to claim these key skills for this coursework depending on how you have completed the tasks and presented your work. Your teacher will need to check your evidence against the key skills specification.

Social and economic factors influencing development

Health, well-being and personal development are affected by a number of important social and economic factors throughout the human life span. People's development is shaped and affected by their personal experience of a variety of social factors such as culture, gender, education and housing. These are outlined in more detail below.

Social factors

Culture

Individual development is influenced by the customs, values, beliefs and way of life of the particular society, or group in society, into which people are born and grow up. These are known as cultural influences. Children are not likely to know that their development is being shaped by cultural influences because they acquire their culture through the ways in which they are brought up and through their experience of the world.

Gender

An individual's sex is a biologically defined characteristic. Physical differences determine whether a person is male or female. Gender, however, is a socially defined characteristic. The qualities and roles that are associated with being masculine or feminine vary between different societies and change over time. For example, it is more acceptable for a man to express caring qualities and still be seen as masculine in the late twentieth century than it was in the 1950s, when this would have been seen to be incompatible with masculinity.

Sex and gender are very closely associated. Girls are expected to take on and express qualities that are socially defined as feminine and boys are generally expected to take on and express a masculine gender identity. These gender expectations influence development because they shape the ways in which men and women experience the world and are treated by others.

Family and friends

The experience of living as part of a family is something that most people have at some time in their life. The family is a very important influence on people's early development, as it is said to carry out primary socialisation. This means that it teaches children the values, beliefs and skills that will prepare them for their adult roles. The family has a vital, ongoing role to play in protecting, providing for and supporting people at various stages of their development.

Education

In the United Kingdom most children go to school between the ages of five and 16 years to receive their formal education. The experience of going to school, and the nature of what is learnt there, tend to have a powerful effect on people's intellectual, social and emotional development. Formal education experiences are part of secondary socialisation

Some people learn a lot at school, are successful in passing examinations and see formal education as a positive influence on their development. A negative experience of formal education can also have an important effect on development.

Housing and environment

◀ A poor standard of housing can adversly affect physical and mental health

Housing provides people with the material, or physical, conditions in which they spend much of their time. The type and standard of housing that people live in is related to their income. People with low incomes are less able to afford a good standard of housing or to be able to maintain it and heat it adequately. Damp, overcrowded and neglected properties provide the kind of conditions in which people are more likely to develop respiratory disorders and infectious diseases, such as tuberculosis and bronchitis.

Families with very low incomes, unable to afford to own or rent their own homes, are now increasingly likely to experience even lower standards of housing in bed and breakfast hotels. People who are homeless and who sleep rough are very prone to poor physical and mental health. They live in a very harsh physical environment and face difficulties in getting the financial and emotional support that they need.

Ethnicity

Ethnicity, like gender, is socially defined. People tend to define their own ethnicity, and that of other people, according to the social characteristics that lead them to belong to a particular community. For example, where people have a shared history or culture, a common geographical origin, a particular skin colour, or a common language or religion they are often seen as having a shared ethnicity. Ethnicity is often an important feature of a person's identity. It may affect personal development because it leads the individual to seek out and take part in particular activities or social groups. It may also be a label (Asian, black, Muslim, Welsh) that influences how other people treat and respond to the person. This in itself can have a powerful effect on personal development.

Isolation

On the whole, people are social animals. Contact with others is important to promote social and emotional development during all of the different life stages. People can become socially isolated because of illness, social exclusion, language or cultural differences. Their isolation will reduce opportunities to develop supportive relationships that would promote personal development. People who experience social isolation may also experience a reduction in their self-esteem and sense of self-worth as a result.

Stereotyping and discrimination

Unfair discrimination occurs when people are treated unequally and unfairly in comparison to others. Age, disability, gender, ethnicity, religion and sexuality are all factors that lead to some people being unfairly discriminated against in the UK. The people who discriminate unfairly tend to do so because they have and express prejudices. A prejudice is a negative or hostile feeling or attitude about something.

When people hold prejudiced views about a group of people they often overgeneralise in a negative way about their characteristics. They then apply these generalisations to all people whom they feel belong to the group. When people are prejudiced they are often prejudiced against specific groups of people, such as gays and lesbians or people of different colour. The process of grouping people together in terms of single dominant characteristics and overgeneralising, rather than acknowledging and appreciating their individual differences, is known as stereotyping.

Stereotyping and unfair discrimination are likely to have a negative effect on people's personal development and self-esteem. They limit an individual's opportunities to really develop and be a unique person and may lead to low self-worth, frustration and a sense of rejection or not fitting in.

Employment

Work, like formal education, is said to be an important contributor to secondary socialisation. People's values, beliefs and attitudes are influenced by the people they work with. Work is also an opportunity to develop new skills and extend physical, intellectual and social abilities. Not having work can also affect an individual's development. The experience of long-term unemployment can have psychological and emotional effects which reduce a person's ability to develop and use their social skills. It may also create financial pressures that influence their development.

Economic factors

Personal development can be affected by a number of key money-related, or economic factors.

Income

Income is the term given to the inflow of money that households receive. People receive money through working, and from pension payments, welfare benefits and other sources such as investments. Money matters in modern life! Studies show that the amount of income people and their families receive, and the things they spend it on, have a big impact on personal development. People who have a very low income and who experience poverty, are most likely to suffer ill health and have their opportunities for personal development restricted.

> Poverty means staying at home, often being bored, not seeing friends, not going to the cinema, not going out for a drink and not being able to take the children out for a trip or a treat or a holiday. It means coping with the stresses of managing on very little money, often for months or even years. It means having to withstand the onslaught of society's pressure to consume ... Above all, poverty takes away the building blocks to create the tools for the future – your "life chances". It steals away the opportunity to have a life unmarked by sickness, a decent education, a secure home and a long retirement. It stops people being able to plan ahead. It stops people being able to take control of their lives.
>
> Oppenheim C and Harker L (1996) *Poverty: The Facts*, 3rd Edition, Child Poverty Action Group.

▶ Children born into poverty
may become trapped in a
cycle of deprivation

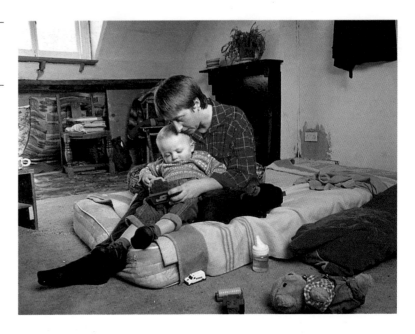

Resources

People who have low incomes can find that their lack of
resources exclude them from the minimum acceptable way of
life of the community in which they live. It is rare, because of
the existence of welfare benefits, for individuals and families in
the United Kingdom not to have enough income for essential
food, clothing and housing. Despite this, there are still
situations in which some people fall through the welfare
benefits safety net and live for periods of time in absolute
poverty. This means that they find themselves without the
basic means to pay for essential items like food, clothing and
housing.

Far more people in the United Kingdom live in relative
poverty and experience social exclusion. Relative poverty
means that a person is poor when compared to most other
people in society. Because of the lack of financial and other
resources, the person finds it difficult to take part in, and
enjoy, the accepted way of life of the community in which he
or she lives. This is known as social exclusion.

Children who are born into families experiencing poverty
may find this difficult to escape from as they become trapped
in a cycle of deprivation that has a powerful effect on their
personal development and life chances.

Build your learning

Summary points

- The ways in which people experience society have a significant effect on their personal development.

- Culture, gender and ethnicity are all social factors that shape personal development and become an important part of individual identity.

- People's experience of education and employment, their membership of, or isolation from, family and friendship groups and the quality of housing and environment that they enjoy, all contribute to their personal development.

- Socialisation, unfair discrimination and stereotyping are all social processes that have an impact on the way in which people develop.

- Lack of money is a key economic factor that restricts opportunities for personal development and that can lead to social exclusion.

Key words and phrases

You should know the meaning of the words and phrases listed below as they relate to the influence of social and economic factors on personal development. If you are not sure about any of them, go back through the last five pages to check and refresh your understanding.

- Culture
- Gender
- Primary socialisation
- Secondary socialisation

- Social factors
- Economic factors
- Ethnicity

- Absolute poverty
- Relative poverty
- Social exclusion

Student questions

1 In your own words, explain how culture influences personal development.

2 Would you classify social and economic factors as nature or nurture influences on development?

3 What key function does the family play in people's early development?

4 How do prejudices lead to unfair discrimination?

5 What is social exclusion?

Development of the self-concept

How we see or think about ourselves is an important influence on our personal development. For example, it has an effect on the way we form, and contribute to, the relationships that we have with other people. If we see or think of ourselves as a popular and likeable person we tend to be more outgoing and confident than if we see ourselves as shy and uninteresting to others.

Making a self-portrait

Think about your main features and characteristics. For example, consider:

- your height

- gender

- eye colour

- where you live

- personality.

Using both words and pictures produce a self-portrait that describes your own view of the essential you at this point in your life.

The self-portrait that you produced in the last activity describes your present self-image.

Assessing your self-esteem

How do you feel about yourself as a person at the moment? Write some comments about the things that you:

- like about yourself at the moment

- would like to change if you could

- are good at

- feel weaker or no good at.

The information that results from questions like those in the last activity, gives an impression of your **self-esteem**. This means the worth, or value, that you, as a person, attribute to yourself and your skills and abilities. People who compare themselves negatively to others, who believe that they are not very good at anything, or who feel criticised, unloved and unimportant to others tend to have low self-esteem. People who are confident, without being arrogant, who accept that they have strengths and weaknesses, and who feel encouraged, loved and wanted, tend not to undervalue themselves so much. Their self-esteem is generally higher as a result.

A person's self-image combines with his or her self-esteem to make up the **self-concept**. This can be described by the formula:

self-concept = self-image + self-esteem

People's self-concept is a central part of their identity. Having a clear, positive picture of who we are and how we feel about ourselves helps to give us a sense of psychological security and affects the way that we relate to other people.

Factors affecting the self-concept

Our self-concept is influenced by the ways others behave towards us, the way that we respond to this and our beliefs about the sort of person we are. A number of factors affect how we, and other people, make decisions about what sort of person we are.

Age, appearance and developmental maturity

The image that you have of yourself today will not be the self-image that you reflect upon when you are forty, sixty or eighty years old. The physical, intellectual and emotional changes that occur as you age and mature will change your self-concept over time. For example, people's self-image is linked to the view that they have of their physical capabilities. Your physical capabilities will change as you experience health, fitness, illness and disability at different points in your life. The value that society attaches to you as an individual will also alter as you grow older. In western societies like ours, old age is generally viewed in a negative way and older people seem to be less valued than young people. The way that people of different ages are portrayed in the media confirms this and inevitably affects the self-concepts of many older people.

Appearance is a factor that is closely related to age when we look at influences on self-concept. People's physical characteristics, the way that they dress and their non-verbal behaviour all influence, and express, features of their self-concept.

Again, the reaction of other people to our appearance affects our self-esteem and self-concept. Some physical characteristics are more valued in our society, and evoke a more positive response than others. How we present ourselves, and how we believe others see us, are important factors influencing our overall self-concept, especially when we are adolescents and young adults. As we get older, physical appearance and the way that we present ourselves tends to have a smaller impact on our self-concept.

Culture

Culture and ethnicity (see pages 204 and 206) affect self-concept by influencing people's feelings of belonging and ideas about membership of different social groups. Culture and ethnic identity can give people a sense of shared values but can also lead to people being treated differently, perhaps in a discriminatory way, and thereby influencing their sense of self-worth.

Environment

Housing, the amount of money a family has and the quality of the physical surroundings in which they live are all features of people's environment. The type of environment into which we are born and develop can influence and shape our self-concepts. Different types of environments give people different opportunities and expose people to different pressures and influences. People growing up in an urban, inner-city environment have different experiences, pressures and opportunities to those of people who grow up in rural, village surroundings.

Education

Educational experiences can have a major impact on people's self-concept. The things that teachers and fellow pupils say, and the way that they treat us, can affect self-image and self-esteem during the life stages of childhood and adolescence when people are very open to suggestions about who and what they are. For some people, educational success helps to form a positive self-image and high self-esteem. For others, school can be a more negative experience that leaves them feeling less capable than others and with a negative view of themselves, their skills and self-worth.

Gender

This term refers to the way ideas about masculinity and femininity are applied to men and women in our society (see page 204). Wider social attitudes towards gender can place pressure on, and shape, people's self-concept. In western

◄ The typical family – a stereotype but not the reality for many families

societies there are a number of gender stereotypes associated with male and female roles and behaviour. The images of men and women presented in the media express these stereotypes and the general social expectations of men and women.

Gender stereotypes do not reflect the reality of the lives of most men and women in British society. Despite this, they can still shape self-image and self-esteem in a positive way, especially where an individual is able, and wishes, to conform to the roles and ways of looking and behaving that the stereotypes suggest. Gender stereotypes can also have a negative effect on self-concept. They can induce guilt, a sense of inadequacy and lack of self-confidence, especially where the person is unable or unwilling to match up to the stereotype of men or women in a particular situation.

Relationships

The relationships that people have, especially through their experience of family life, during education and at work, have a powerful effect on their self-concept. Family relationships play a critical role in shaping the self-concept. Early relationships are built on effective attachments to parents and close family members, and the sense of security and being loved that comes from these bonds. Poor family relationships can have a lasting effect on the self-concept.

During adolescence and adulthood, people go through a number of phases of emotional and sexual development as they experience friendships and more intimate relationships with non-family members. Simply because they grow older, and mature emotionally, people also adapt their outlook and behaviour to take account of the thoughts and feelings that they have. For example, young people who may have had a strong image of themselves as young, free and single learn new things about themselves and have to adapt their self-concept when they form an intimate, long-term partnership or get married.

Build your learning

Summary points

- Self-concept is a central part of an individual's sense of identity.

- Self-concept is a combination of how people see themselves (self-image) and what they feel about themselves (self-esteem).

- Social factors, such as culture, education and gender, maturation and the relationships that people experience with others all shape their self-concept in a continuous developmental process.

Key words and phrases

You should know the meaning of the words and phrases listed below as they relate to the development of the self-concept. If you are not sure about any of them, go back through the last five pages to check and refresh your understanding.

- **Self-image**
- **Self-concept**
- **Culture**
- **Self-esteem**
- **Relationships**
- **Gender**
- **Stereotype**

Student questions

1 Why might a person have low self-esteem?

2 During which life stages does appearance seem to be a particularly strong feature of the self-concept?

3 How can educational experiences affect the self-concept?

4 What is a gender stereotype?

5 What effects can gender stereotypes have on the development of the self-concept?

ASSESSMENT WORK

Influences on the development of the self-concept

The self-concept is a combination of the image that people have of themselves, how they value themselves as a person, and their beliefs about how others see and value them as a person. The self-concept develops throughout the life cycle but becomes more important and sensitive during adolescence and early adulthood when individuals are seeking to establish their sense of personal identity.

You are asked to explore the development of the self-concept as part of the end of unit assignment. The box below outlines what you need to do to give yourself a chance of gaining a pass, merit or distinction grade.

	Assessment criteria	Which tasks do I need to do?
Pass	Describe clearly the social and economic factors that affect the development and self-concept of a person in the case studies.	6a
Merit	Correctly relate physical, social and economic effects to personal development and self-concept. Analyse positive and negative effects of personal relationships on an individual's development and self-concept.	6b 6c
Distinction	Consider which factor has had the most significant influence on the development and self-concept of one person in the case studies.	6d

To complete the tasks that follow you will need to either:

- use your own experiences and write about yourself, or

- persuade somebody else to let you talk to him or her about his or her personal development and self-concept.

When you have decided, work through as many of the tasks as you can.

What to do

(6a) Using examples, describe clearly the social and economic factors (such as culture, gender, family, friends, education, ethnicity, and environment) that influenced the development of the individual's self-concept.

(6b) Explain how physical, social and economic factors have combined to influence the personal development and self-concept of the individual.

(6c) Find out and explain how the individual's development and self-concept has been affected by different personal relationships (family, friends, colleagues) during his or her life so far. You should explain the positive and negative effects of different personal relationships on the individual's development and self-concept.

(6d) Which factor has had the most significant influence on the development and self-concept of the individual? You should explain why the factor you've identified is the key to understanding his or her pattern of development and self-concept.

Key skills

C2.1a, C2.2, C2.3, IT2.2, IT2.3

It may be possible to claim these key skills for this coursework depending on how you have completed the tasks and presented your work. Your teacher will need to check your evidence against the key skills specification.

You might, for example, choose an elderly relative or friend of the family. In undertaking task 6b, about physical, social and economic effects, your subject may describe the lack of money that his or her parents had in the 1930s, how this led to food shortages and a lack of new clothes. This in turn may have affected his or her physical growth (lack of food) and self-concept (being poor). He or she may have felt less valued than wealthy children who did have new shoes and clothes and plenty to eat. (Of course, the opposite may have been true – he or she may have been one of the wealthy children at the time!)

Life changes and life events

A life event is an incident or experience that has a major impact on the direction or quality of an individual's life and personal development. Every person's life changes as a result of the significant events and experiences that happen as he or she passes through each life stage. Some of the life events that shape or alter the pattern of a person's life are predictable, such as the birth of a baby. Others, such as sudden illness, are unpredictable.

Predictable life events

In western societies there are a number of predictable life events that are expected milestones in people's social and personal development and which occur at predictable points in the life cycle. Some of these are described below.

Starting school

This is one of the first predictable life events. Beginning primary school is a turning point in children's lives. It involves spending time away from their parents and introduces them to a wider circle of people and to new patterns of behaviour. For many children this predictable life event is initially difficult to deal with. It is eventually successful because of the support received from parents, brothers and sisters and teachers. At eleven years old most children change from primary to secondary school. This change can be as difficult to adjust to as starting primary school was at a younger age.

▶ Will Ffion and Rhian remain close friends now that they no longer attend the same school?

Changing schools

Ffion Robbins is 11 years old. She lives in a small village in North Wales with her parents and two younger brothers Tom, aged eight, and Geraint, aged six. Her grandparents live ten miles away and are regular visitors. Ffion is about to finish at Wylfa Primary School and move to Glan Aber Comprehensive School in September. She knows everyone at Wylfa, as all the children come from the same village and her teachers have been there since she started. She doesn't want to leave her primary school and admits to being scared of going to the big school, as she calls it, eight miles away. Ffion's best friend at school, Rhian, goes to swimming club with her, and belongs to the same church group. Rhian will be going to a different school in September.

1 Describe the ways in which this transition in Ffion's life might affect her in the next few months.

2 What type of help and support might she need as she experiences this change in her life?

3 If you were one of Ffion's parents, what would you tell her about the likely impact of changing schools on her friendship with Rhian?

Starting work

Starting work is another predictable life event for most people. In the United Kingdom, schooling is compulsory up to the age of 16, though the majority of young people don't leave school until they are older than this. Nevertheless, everybody finishes school and studying at some point in their life. Starting work places different responsibilities and expectations on people. It is a point at which young people, as workers, are required to behave more independently, without the support of parents and teachers.

Leaving home

Leaving home is a major transition in life that happens for most people in their late teens or early twenties. As young people establish more personal and financial independence from their parents, they usually broaden their social relationships, find work or take up a place on an educational course in a different part of the country. They reach a point where they either choose to, or have to, leave home. For some young people this transition is the point at which they feel they have established their independence. For others, the changes that result from leaving home are not as positive. Their experiences can include loneliness, lack of support and poverty. Whether the consequences are initially positive or negative, the experience of leaving home is a major event that will always be memorable for many people.

Marriage

Marriage is a life event that is generally viewed positively and which is celebrated by thousands of people each year. It involves a major adaptation in personal relationships and behaviour for the couple. Ideally, it establishes a deeper emotional and psychological commitment between them. Marriages also alter family relationships. The roles of family members change and new members are introduced into family groups. For example, in-laws become part of a wider family network and relationships between original family members may weaken because of the practicalities of a son or daughter moving away to live with his or her new partner.

▶ Marriage can alter the balance of family relationships

Having children

Having children leads to major changes in people's lives. Parenthood involves a change in role for both partners in a relationship and introduces new personal responsibilities and financial pressures. Decisions must be made about how to bring up the child, about how the work involved should be divided and about the need to provide ongoing, nurturing love and financial support for the child. This can be seen to offer positive, enjoyable experiences but can also seem a burden and create a lot of stress at times.

Moving home

Moving home is recognised as a stressful life event for many people. Home is usually a place that people associate with safety, security and stability in their lives. Moving home means a break with the past and perhaps with friends, neighbours and the security of familiar surroundings. The practical demands of organising the removal of possessions, arranging finance to cover the cost of moving, and perhaps buying a house or flat, add to the emotional strain associated with this life event.

Retirement

Retirement is the point at which people end their working career. In the United Kingdom, the retirement age for men is currently 65 and for women 60 years of age. Retirement is a major predictable change that requires an adjustment in daily routine, that means an alteration in status and that has an impact on people's social relationships and financial situation. For people who have been very committed to their work, and whose work provided their social life, retirement can give them too much time to fill. Retirement can also cause financial problems. State and occupational pensions are likely to provide less money than a salary. For many older people, retirement can be the beginning of financial hardship. For other people who have planned for their retirement and who have other interests and friendships, retirement can offer new opportunities and be welcomed as a positive life event.

Death

Death is inevitable. It is the final predictable life event for all of us because we all know that one day each of our lives must end. What we don't usually know, is which day this will be! Most people expect and hope to die painlessly in old age. The impact of a person's death will be felt by those who have had family, personal, work and friendship relationships with him or her. Death is acknowledged by all religious faiths through rituals and services, like funerals and wakes, which celebrate the life and achievements of the dead person.

Unexpected life events

Not all of the major events that shape and change our lives are predictable. Life events such as serious illness, disability, divorce and bereavement can happen unexpectedly to anyone.

Events like these can have a major effect on people's lives. They can result in significant change, or a transition point, occurring. **Unexpected life events** are usually thought of as negative, but can sometimes lead to positive change in a person's life.

Serious illness

Serious illness can be a major, but unexpected, event in an individual's life. It can result in massive changes to the person's whole lifestyle as he or she tries to cope with the effects of the illness. People who experience serious illnesses, such as heart attacks, multiple sclerosis or cancer, may find themselves unable to carry out their usual daily routines and can find that their relationships with others change because of their illness. People who experience a serious illness may need additional practical help and emotional support from close relatives and friends and may lose some of their independence. For partners and close relatives, the person's illness may be the thing around which they organise their own time, lifestyle and relationship with the person.

Disability

Disability can be inherited and present from birth, or can be caused by accident or because of a person's lifestyle. For example, people who drink too much alcohol may acquire a disability as a result of being involved in a road traffic accident or a fight or because of the direct effects of large amounts of alcohol on the body.

People with disabilities must adapt their skills and lifestyle to cope with the everyday situations that they face. A disability can cause practical problems, such as not being able to move, pick up and hold things or manage personal hygiene and toilet needs independently. It may also result in psychological stress and alter the person's personal relationships. Friends, family and colleagues are likely to be affected by disability. They will need to adjust their relationship with the person to take account of the disabled person's new situation.

Divorce

Divorce is an unexpected life event. It has an impact on the couple themselves and on those who are part of a family that has resulted from the couple's marriage. People do not marry intending to get divorced, but divorce is now relatively common in the United Kingdom.

The breakdown of a marriage, and the process of going through a divorce have an emotional impact on the couple concerned and financial and practical consequences. Separation will probably mean having to find different accommodation and independent sources of income. Where the couple have children, the impact of their divorce will be felt by the children because of new living arrangements, changing relationships and sometimes the need to adapt to new step-parents.

Redundancy

Redundancy happens when an employer decides that a job is no longer required and ends the contract of employment of the person who does that job. It is different to dismissal or sacking, as people who are made redundant lose their jobs through no fault of their own. Because of rapid changes in the way that businesses are run and recent economic recessions, redundancy has become a much more common experience. It can have a major impact as people lose their salary and find their financial situation suddenly insecure. It may break up firm friendships and also leave people feeling as though they have no clear or valued role in life.

Bereavement

Bereavement is the term given to the deep feelings of loss that people experience when a person to whom they are emotionally attached dies or goes out of their life in another way, such as through divorce or the ending of a long-term relationship. The death of some people may be anticipated and prepared for because of their greater age or because they have a terminal illness. While the loss of a loved one can sometimes be anticipated, it may still be hard to accept and deal with emotionally. Bereavement can be even more traumatic and psychologically difficult when a person's death is unexpected and occurs suddenly or dramatically, for example, because of an accident, serious injury or suicide. A sense of bereavement can cause those who remain both short and long-term problems in accepting and adjusting to the loss of the person concerned.

◀ Many people find it difficult to cope with bereavement

Predictable or unpredictable?

Which of the following life events are predictable and which are unpredictable? Make a list.

1 Becoming a parent	7 Leaving home	13 Losing your job
2 Starting school	8 Getting divorced	14 Learning to read
3 Getting married	9 Retiring from work	15 Going into care
4 Getting your first job	10 Going bankrupt	16 Winning the Lottery
5 Being promoted	11 Taking exams	17 Being kidnapped
6 Moving to a new house	12 The death of a loved one	18 Getting a nursing qualification

Life stages	Life events
Infancy to childhood	
Adolescence	
Adulthood	
Midlife	
Old age	

At what life stage are the above life events most likely to occur? Match them on the lifeline.

Types of support

Major events in people's lives such as going to school, starting work, marriage, divorce and bereavement all mean experiencing change. For people to benefit from the changes that major events offer, they need to work out ways of coping and adapting. There are a number of common methods of managing change, including using **family support** and **social support** and seeking **professional help** where necessary.

Family support

Family support is often the first form of help that people seek when they experience a major life event. Families may be able to provide practical and emotional support at times of stress, change and crisis and are the source of a lot of informal care for people in all age groups. People need support from their families at different stages in their lives. Marriage is a major life event in which people may be supported emotionally and financially by their parents. Similarly, parenthood and bereavement are occasions when family members may need to support each other emotionally and financially.

Social support

Social support is useful in enabling people to adapt to the personal and emotional changes that a major life event can cause. It may take the form of practical help and advice from people such as work colleagues and friends. Social support may also be offered by voluntary workers from organisations such as the Citizens Advice Bureau, Relate (the marriage guidance agency) and MIND (the mental health charity). These organisations enable people to obtain information and guidance and provide opportunities for people to talk through the different options available to them.

◀ Citizens Advice Bureaux throughout the country offer support and advice free of charge

Professional support can be obtained from health and social care workers who are trained and qualified to deal with the complex difficulties that families and friends are unable to help with. Where people need financial help and advice, support is available from professionally qualified advisers, banks, building societies and government departments such as the Department of Social Security.

Identifying support needs

Our reactions to change are important as they affect our health and well-being. Identify ways of coping with the changes that may result from each of the major life events listed below. Write down examples of the three types of support that you might need to cope with each situation.

- The break up of a marriage or long-term relationship.

- Leaving school or college with no job to go to.

- Moving to a new area of the country with your family.

- Being involved in a car crash.

- Losing your sight.

- Being promoted to a very responsible position at work.

- Leaving home to go to university or to live with friends.

- The birth of your first child.

- Being made redundant.

- Failing to get the exam grades that are needed for a job.

- The death of a close relative or friend.

- Being diagnosed with a serious illness.

- The onset of puberty.

- Winning the National Lottery jackpot.

- Being sent to prison.

- Starting employment.

- Moving from primary to secondary school.

- Getting married.

- Getting into serious debt.

- One of your parents developing Alzheimer's disease.

- Retiring from work after 40 years in the same job.

Discuss your ideas with a partner, explaining the reasons for your decisions.

Build your learning

Summary points

- Life events are incidents or experiences that play a central part in how people develop.

- Life events can be predictable transitions, such as starting school or retiring from work, or unexpected events, such as serious illness or bereavement.

- Life events occur throughout the life span and tend to have a significant emotional impact.

- People cope with life events by using family, social and professional support.

Key words and phrases

You should know the meaning of the words and phrases listed below as they relate to life events and their impact on development. If you are not sure about any of them, go back through the last nine pages to check and refresh your understanding.

- **Life event**
- **Social support**
- **Retirement**
- **Redundancy**
- **Professional support**
- **Voluntary workers**
- **Predictable life event**
- **Unpredictable life event**

Student questions

1 Name three predictable life events that occur before an individual reaches adulthood.

2 Explain why getting married can be a major life event that strongly influences personal development.

3 What is the difference between retirement and redundancy?

4 What happens when a person experiences a bereavement?

5 Which organisation offers support to people who are experiencing marital or relationship problems?

ASSESSMENT WORK

Life changes and types of support

Predictable and unexpected events can change people's lives and are an important influence on development. When major events occur in people's lives, their ability to cope can be affected by the types of support that are available to them. As part of your end of unit assignment you are required to show an understanding of life changing events and types of support. The box below outlines what you need to do to give yourself a chance of gaining a pass, merit or distinction grade.

	Assessment criteria	Which tasks do I need to do?
Pass	Describe relevant support provided to an individual through expected life changes.	7a 7b
Merit	Use relevant examples to analyse how support provided can assist individuals through expected and unexpected life changes.	7c
Distinction	Analyse the different ways in which people cope with change and how these changes could affect the type of help and support they need.	7d

As in the previous assessment work activity on page 216, you need to decide where you will get your information for this activity. You can either use your own experience of life events and types of support or you can obtain information from a volunteer. When you've decided, work through as many of the following tasks as you can.

What to do

7a Briefly describe the major life events that have influenced the personal development of an individual.

7b Identify the types of help or support that the person who experienced these life events received, or could have benefited from.

7c How can support assist individuals through expected and unexpected life changes? Describe a specific life event, the type of support that might help and its effects on the individual.

7d Identify a number of different ways in which people might cope with the changes you describe above. Explain how different ways of reacting to change can affect the types of help and support that people need.

Self-assessment of evidence

What to do

To complete Unit 3 you need to produce a report on human development based on one or more case studies. Your report must include work on:

- characteristics of different life stages
- factors that have affected personal development and self-concept
- the changes which have happened in a person's life
- examples of support used by an individual in the case studies.

If you have completed assessment work activities 1 to 7, you should have produced enough work for your report. You should organise the work that you've completed into a report format. Ideally, your report should have:

- a cover and contents list
- an introduction, explaining what the report is all about
- a section on the physical characteristics of each life stage (assessment work 1, 2, 3, 4 and 5)
- a section on the self-concept (assessment work 6)
- a section on life changes and support (assessment work 7).

What can you achieve?

By checking through the work you've done you can self-assess your evidence before your teacher or lecturer marks and grades it and work out what grade you may be able to achieve.

You must complete all of the 'pass grade' activities to complete the unit. If you want to try and get a merit you must complete all of the pass grade activities and all of the merit grade activities. For a distinction you must complete every activity. When you hand in your work your teacher or lecturer will mark it and decide whether you have met the assessment criteria and reached the required standard.

Page	Activity	Grade	Have I completed this? (Tick)
181	1a, 1b, 1c	Pass	☐
186	2a, 2b, 2c	Pass	☐
193	3a, 3b, 3c	Pass	☐
198	4a, 4b, 4c	Pass	☐
203	5a, 5b, 5c	Pass	☐
216	6a	Pass	☐
216	6b	Merit	☐
216	6c	Merit	☐
216	6d	Distinction	☐
228	7a	Pass	☐
228	7b	Pass	☐
228	7c	Merit	☐
228	7d	Distinction	☐

It's good being with the children, but it's hard work as well because you can't just stop for a break or stop watching them.

I told the matron that I didn't want to do the ironing each week. She said that I had to, so I called my tutor who got me another, better placement.

Thursdays at placement are my favourite part of the course.

Placement's good because you get to learn practical things about care work. When I finish the GNVQ course, I'd like to get a job in the nursery where I go for work placement.

Sometimes it's hard to know what you're supposed to do, especially at the beginning. You do get used to it and get to know people quite quickly though. All the children and some of the parents knew my name by the end and I didn't want to leave.

I've worked with children in a nursery, the elderly in a residential home and with a pharmacist in a hospital. The hospital was my favourite placement.

Work placement in a care setting

The GNVQ Intermediate Health and Social Care course is a vocational course. It is designed to provide students with opportunities to develop knowledge and basic skills relevant to care work. One of the key differences between a GNVQ course and an academic course, like GCSE, is the use of work placements. These enable students to experience the real world of vocational work and are a very important part of any vocational course.

This appendix gives guidance on your work placement. It offers advice about choosing your work placement and suggests ways of benefitting most from the experience.

What are work placements?

Work placements are usually arranged and supported by the teachers or lecturers who run your GNVQ Intermediate Health and Social Care course. They involve you spending time working under the supervision of permanent staff in a care setting such as a nursery, infant school, or nursing home.

Students typically spend one day a week in a work placement for most of a term and then have a block placement where they work for up to five days a week for two or three weeks in their final term. Schools and colleges have different ways of organising work placements. It is best to try and gain experience of working in a couple of different care settings during your course. This will give you experience of working with client groups who have different sorts of needs, like children and older people, and different groups of staff who use different skills and practices in their work.

The importance of work experience

Some students who take GNVQ Intermediate Health and Social Care courses may have already gained some experience of working in care settings, through previous work experience whilst at school or through part-time jobs. Many students have no practical experience other than looking after their younger brothers or sisters or the children of relatives and neighbours as an informal carer. Regardless of previous experience, you can gain a great deal from the work placements that are a part of your course.

Work placements are important because they:

- give you the chance to experience the real world of care work and understand what is involved in caring for other people
- enable you to develop basic skills in care practice
- give you a chance to explore different kinds of care work before you make a decision about the kind of job you would like to apply for when your course ends
- provide you with an opportunity to apply what you've learnt in school or college to work with real patients and clients
- give you a chance to gain confidence in working with others in care settings
- provide you with a chance to assess your own strengths and abilities as well as the areas where you need to develop your skills for care work.

Choosing a work placement

You may already have some preferences for the type of work placement that you want to have during your GNVQ Intermediate Health and Social Care course. The types of work placement that are available tend to include:

- residential care homes for older people, children, people with mental health problems and people with learning disabilities
- day centres for people with disabilities, older people and children
- nurseries, playgroups and crèches for children under five
- infant classes in primary schools
- hospital wards for older people and children.

The placements for you to choose from will depend on what is available in your local area, the ability of local organisations to provide you with appropriate support and supervision and the contacts your school or college has with care organisations. If you have a particular type of placement in mind, or even a specific organisation in which you'd like to work, you should discuss this with your teacher or tutor to see whether it would be possible to arrange a placement there.

When you are considering the sort of work placement that you would like, think about the answers to the following questions.

- Do you have any previous experience that you'd like to build on?
- What areas do you have a special interest in or preference for?
- Do you have a preference for working with a particular client group?
- Would you benefit from gaining experience in working with a new client group?
- What would you want to get out of a work placement?
- What does your teacher or lecturer think would be a good placement for you at this stage?
- Will the staff who work in the placement organisation be able to provide you with enough help and support?
- Will you be able to get to the work placement on time and without it costing you too much?

Preparing for a work placement

It is always best to work with your teacher or tutor to discuss and arrange an appropriate work placement. When this is confirmed, try to visit, and even have an interview with a member of staff, to check that what you expect of the work placement and the staff who work there matches what is possible and on offer. Finding out about the client group you will be working with, reading any information about the care organisation and reminding yourself of the health and safety duties (see page 133–4) that you and the care organisation have, will all help you to prepare for your work placement.

Expectations

When your work placement has been organised, you should be given the name of a member of staff whom you should contact. It is always a good idea to arrange to go to the work placement before you officially start in order to:

- find out who your supervisor will be, and ideally meet him or her
- agree your start and finish times
- talk about what you expect to be doing during the placement and what you are not expecting to do
- find out what your supervisor expects from you
- find out who you should report to on the first day.

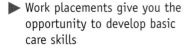

▶ Work placements give you the opportunity to develop basic care skills

Dress and appearance

A member of staff at your work placement will probably tell you about the dress code that you are expected to follow whilst you work there. If you are required to wear a uniform, the placement organisation will usually provide this. It is important that you dress and present yourself in an appropriate way. Clothes that are modest and comfortable, clean and tidy will usually be acceptable. Care work is practical and requires you to wear practical, comfortable clothes and shoes.

The make-up and jewellery that you wish to wear should be acceptable to, and appropriate for, the clients and type of work you will be involved with. Children like to pull shiny earrings and older people may find your nose, eyebrow or other body piercing off-putting. It may be better not to wear either on work placement. Remember that a work placement in a care setting is not a social occasion that people dress up for.

Learning and developing basic care skills

One of the main purposes of undertaking a work placement is to give you the opportunity to experience the real world of care and to develop basic care skills. You should be supported by an experienced care worker who tells you about different tasks and skills, demonstrates what he or she expects you to do and supports you in your efforts to develop good skills. It is important to listen to, observe and ask questions of experienced staff. Requesting help when you need it will usually gain you respect rather than criticism. Avoid attempting tasks or taking on responsibility for things that you are not trained for or do not feel confident about. It is always best to say that you need help and support when this is the case.

In the early stages of your career in care you are likely to make some mistakes. You may have felt confident about completing a particular task that later went wrong or you may do something that you later realise you could have done better or that you are worried about. It is always best to admit your mistakes and let someone else know what has gone wrong. It is possible to learn from your mistakes and you should never keep quiet if somebody else might suffer harm because of them. Don't let early mistakes get you down too much. Most good care workers will admit that they have made mistakes at some time in their career and have been successful because they learnt from them.

Working with others

Care work is all about working with other people. The relationships that you develop with members of staff and clients are a very important aspect of your work placement. You will be attending your work placement organisation for a limited period of time. Being friendly, approachable and helpful will enhance your relationships with others. Be careful about getting too involved with clients as you have to leave when your placement is over. This might become a difficult situation if a client has become too attached to you.

Most members of staff and clients are very helpful and supportive of students on work placement. There are occasions when a student has a difficult time with a particular member of staff or client. If this happens to you, it is best to inform your supervisor and teacher or tutor to discuss the problem with them as soon as possible.

Good luck with your work placements. Learning in practical care settings is as important as learning in school or college. Many students feel that their work placements are the best part of their courses. Always try to do your best for your patients and clients and don't forget about your own health and well-being and that of your colleagues.

Index

Numbers in green show the page on which the word is defined or used as a key word.